9/8/11

Slavery

Other Books of Related Interest:

At Issue Series

Affirmative Action

Current Controversies Series

Aid To Africa

The Arms Trade

Global Viewpoints Series

Child Labor

Opposing Viewpoints Series

India

Russia

GLOBALVIEWPOINTS

Slavery

Maria Tenaglia-Webster, Book Editor

WILLOW INTERNATIONAL LIBRARY

GREENHAVEN PRESS
A part of Gale, Cengage Learning

GALE
CENGAGE Learning™

Detroit • New York • San Francisco • New Haven, Conn • Waterville, Maine • London

Christine Nasso, *Publisher*
Elizabeth Des Chenes, *Managing Editor*

© 2009 Greenhaven Press, a part of Gale, Cengage Learning

Gale and Greenhaven Press are registered trademarks used herein under license.

For more information, contact:
Greenhaven Press
27500 Drake Rd.
Farmington Hills, MI 48331-3535
Or you can visit our Internet site at gale.cengage.com

For product information and technology assistance, contact us at

Gale Customer Support, 1-800-877-4253
For permission to use material from this text or product, submit all requests online at www.cengage.com/permissions

Further permissions questions can be emailed to permissionrequest@cengage.com

Articles in Greenhaven Press anthologies are often edited for length to meet page requirements. In addition, original titles of these works are changed to clearly present the main thesis and to explicitly indicate the author's opinion. Every effort is made to ensure that Greenhaven Press accurately reflects the original intent of the authors. Every effort has been made to trace the owners of copyrighted material.

Cover image by Sandro Tucci/Time Life Pictures/Getty Images.

LIBRARY OF CONGRESS CATALOGING-IN-PUBLICATION DATA

Slavery / Maria Tenaglia-Webster, book editor.
    p. cm. -- (Global viewpoints)
    Includes bibliographical references and index.
    ISBN 978-0-7377-4472-9 (hardcover)
    ISBN 978-0-7377-4473-6 (pbk.)
    1. Slavery. 2. Prostitution. 3. Child labor. 4. Child abuse. I. Tenaglia-Webster, Maria.
    HT871.S545 2009
    306.3'62--dc22

                                                    2009016630

Printed in the United States of America
1 2 3 4 5 6 7 13 12 11 10 09

Contents

Chapter 1: The Legacy of Slavery

Chapter 2: Slavery in Modern Times

Chapter 3: The Global Problem of Sex Slavery

Chapter 4: The Harsh Reality of Child Slavery

Foreword

"The problems of all of humanity can only be solved by all of humanity."
—*Swiss author Friedrich Dürrenmatt*

Global interdependence has become an undeniable reality. Mass media and technology have increased worldwide access to information and created a society of global citizens. Understanding and navigating this global community is a challenge, requiring a high degree of information literacy and a new level of learning sophistication.

Building on the success of its flagship series, *Opposing Viewpoints*, Greenhaven Press has created the *Global Viewpoints* series to examine a broad range of current, often controversial topics of worldwide importance from a variety of international perspectives. Providing students and other readers with the information they need to explore global connections and think critically about worldwide implications, each *Global Viewpoints* volume offers a panoramic view of a topic of widespread significance.

Drugs, famine, immigration—a broad, international treatment is essential to do justice to social, environmental, health, and political issues such as these. Junior high, high school, and early college students, as well as general readers, can all use *Global Viewpoints* anthologies to discern the complexities relating to each issue. Readers will be able to examine unique national perspectives while, at the same time, appreciating the interconnectedness that global priorities bring to all nations and cultures.

Material in each volume is selected from a diverse range of sources, including journals, magazines, newspapers, nonfiction books, speeches, government documents, pamphlets, organization newsletters, and position papers. *Global Viewpoints* is truly global, with material drawn primarily from international sources available in English and secondarily from U.S. sources with extensive international coverage.

Features of each volume in the *Global Viewpoints* series include:

- An **annotated table of contents** that provides a brief summary of each essay in the volume, including the name of the country or area covered in the essay.

- An **introduction** specific to the volume topic.

- A **world map** to help readers locate the countries or areas covered in the essays.

- For each viewpoint, an **introduction** that contains notes about the author and source of the viewpoint explains why material from the specific country is being presented, summarizes the main points of the viewpoint, and offers three **guided reading questions** to aid in understanding and comprehension.

- **For further discussion** questions that promote critical thinking by asking the reader to compare and contrast aspects of the viewpoints or draw conclusions about perspectives and arguments.

- A worldwide list of **organizations to contact** for readers seeking additional information.

- A **periodical bibliography** for each chapter and a **bibliography of books** on the volume topic to aid in further research.

- A comprehensive **subject index** to offer access to people, places, events, and subjects cited in the text, with the countries covered in the viewpoints highlighted.

Global Viewpoints is designed for a broad spectrum of readers who want to learn more about current events, history, political science, government, international relations, economics, environmental science, world cultures, and sociology—students doing research for class assignments or debates, teachers and faculty seeking to supplement course materials, and others wanting to understand current issues better. By presenting how people in various countries perceive the root causes, current consequences, and proposed solutions to worldwide challenges, *Global Viewpoints* volumes offer readers opportunities to enhance their global awareness and their knowledge of cultures worldwide.

Introduction

> *"The essence of all slavery consists in tak-
> ing the product of another's labor by
> force. It is immaterial whether this force
> be founded upon ownership of the slave
> or ownership of the money that he must
> get to live."*
>
> —*Leo Tolstoy,*
> *nineteenth century Russian novelist*

Virtually every human civilization has been founded on a social hierarchy, and in each case, this hierarchy has addressed the need for laborers to produce goods necessary for the civilization's way of life. From the beginning of recorded history, one form of this contract has been a strict separation of masters and slaves. In one of the oldest written laws, the Babylonian Code of Hammurabi, slave ownership was a serious matter. Leonard W. King's translation of the stone states, "If any one take a male or female slave of the court, or a male or female slave of a freed man, outside the city gates, he shall be put to death." The tendency to slavery is an undeniable part of our past, and it is also a part of our present.

Historically, many societies considered freedom and labor to be completely separate human conditions, so it was a paradox for anyone to be a laborer and also to be free. We can clearly observe slavery in both ancient Greece and the Roman Empire. In Book I of *Aristotle's Politics: A Treatise on Government*, Aristotle sums up the condition of slavery, writing, "therefore a master is only the master of the slave, but no part of him, but the slave is not only the slave of the master but nothing else but that." According to Thomas Wiedemann's *Greek and Roman Slavery*, besides the more common source of slavery—the capture of military prisoners—voluntary debt bondage appeared in the Roman Empire. In this variation on traditional slave ownership, regular citizens resigned themselves to slavery because they could not repay their debts. Throughout the western world in the Middle and Renaissance Ages, most nations practiced slavery, or serfdom—a slave-like condition in which a man is bonded to his feudal master, obligated by law to serve him, even though he is not considered property.

The year 1441 marked the beginning of the exportation of slave labor from Africa, initially by the Portuguese. Over the course of the next three centuries, Africa became the primary source of slave labor for western civilization, especially for the Americas, including the North American colonies, South America, and the Caribbean Islands. This is the historical period most commonly associated with slavery, because it was occurring as recently as two hundred years ago, and because its consequences still linger today. The triangular system that moved money, goods, and slaves among Europe, Africa, and the colonies was called the Atlantic Slave Trade. The European traders would exchange local goods with African kings in exchange for laborers. The laborers were transported to the Americas and exchanged for sugar, tobacco, and other plantation crops. Then those goods were returned to Europe, and the trading began again.

Economically and politically, for the Europeans and Americans, the trade was a tremendous success. It was immensely profitable, bringing wealth to Europe and much-needed labor to the colonies. As argued in *Terms of Labor: Slavery, Serfdom, and Free Labor*, mathematical calculations suggest—especially in the Southern colonies' plantations—that the amount of cheap land necessitated slave labor because there were not enough free men available to sustain plantation operations. Many historians believe that slave labor played a large part in establishing the global dominance of the western nations.

The slave trade had other repercussions for Africa. The most obvious effect was the immediate thinning of the population. Advocates of slave reparations are quick to point out that the population still suffers today. According to Basil Davidson's *The African Slave Trade*, of the geographic area that was hit the hardest by slave traders, "the density is seldom more than ten to a square mile and is often less than one or two." A more subtle side effect is that industry and innovation in African countries suffered greatly and often ceased entirely. Today, much of Africa consists of third world countries, and some scholars believe that the loss of the strongest members of its population contributed to its hardships.

By the eighteenth century, the concept of workers' rights and a laboring middle class took root in western law and moral attitudes. "Free labor" was established in Europe and America, wherein "freemen" worked for, but were not legally bound to, their employers. Workers had unprecedented rights, and their living conditions improved. With this change, public opinion slowly shifted in favor of abolition to end slavery. Beginning with the historic *Somersett* case in Great Britain in 1772, which held that slavery was unlawful in England, judges began to set legal precedents to support human rights for slaves.

In response to a large revolt among slaves, known as the Haitian Revolution (from 1791–1804), France abolished slavery in 1794, although it was reinstated again in 1802 and finally abolished in 1848. British politician William Wilberforce led the antislavery movement in England, helping to persuade Parliament to pass a bill in 1807 outlawing slave trade, and supporting the campaign that led to complete abolition throughout the British Empire in 1833. Correspondingly, within this time frame, other nations were gradually making attempts to abolish slavery as well, including Argentina, Gran Colombia (the region that today includes Ecuador, Colombia, and Venezuela), Greece, Chile, Mexico, Bolivia, Denmark, and the Netherlands. In the United States, a tendency toward abolitionist policies triggered the civil war, and in 1865, the 13th Amendment formally abolished slavery.

Many are surprised to learn that although slavery is internationally outlawed, it is still thriving in today's global economy. New forms of slavery appear in third world and developed countries alike. Human trafficking has become big business globally. According to the Council of Europe's Marta Requena, as cited in the *International Herald Tribune*, "the profits are very high, and the risks are very low," with a global annual market at around €32 billion (US$42.5 billion) estimated in the 2006 article "Council of Europe Says Human Trafficking Has Reached 'Epidemic Proportions.'" Trafficking victims are recruited through deception, force, and even abduction. Modern-day slavery victims include indentured servants, exploited migrant laborers, sex workers forced into prostitution, and child slaves.

Global Viewpoints: Slavery examines contemporary issues regarding the bondage of individuals against their free will. The authors investigate how countries are contending with the historical legacy of slavery from generations past, and explore the problems associated with slavery in the modern world. Like those held in bondage throughout history, today's slaves labor to bring profits to their masters, with little hope of finding freedom.

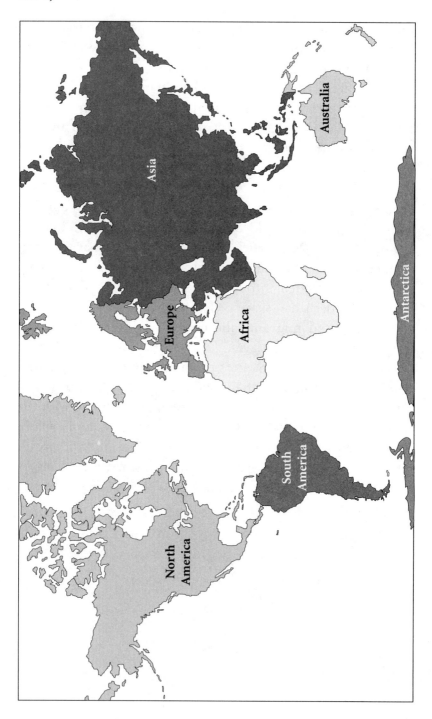

GLOBAL VIEWPOINTS

CHAPTER 1

The Legacy of Slavery

Regret and Redemption for Slavery's Past

Deep Kisor Datta-Ray

In the following viewpoint, author Deep Kisor Datta-Ray argues that empty apologies accomplish very little. Rather than mending slave trade injustices, such apologies instead pull attention away from the problems of today. In addition, calculating reparations would "demand an impossible balance sheet," the author believes, pointing out that lessons from history should help drive efforts to fight racism and modern-day exploitations. Based in London, Datta-Ray is a historian and commentator on Asian affairs.

As you read, consider the following questions:

1. What year did Britain pass the Abolition Act, banning the trade of slaves?
2. Why does the author consider President George W. Bush's slavery apology ineffective?
3. According to the author, why would follow-up actions, such as reparations, be difficult?

Japanese Prime Minister Shinzo Abe's apology for his nation's wartime sex abuse in China, Korea and elsewhere will encourage those who are celebrating the 200th anniversary of the abolition of slavery by demanding a formal apology. The

Deep Kisor Datta-Ray, "Going Beyond 'Sorry,'" *South China Morning Post*, April 4, 2007, p. A15. www.sussex.ac.uk. Reproduced by permission.

sentiment is understandable and reparation should be made, wherever possible. But the assumption that a simple "sorry" absolves past injustice makes light of slavery and exploits history to distract attention from today's wrongs.

The slavery debate is organised around two opposing narratives. On one side, the apology lobby argues that the Atlantic slave trade between Africa, Britain and America was a uniquely and absolutely immoral process whereby whites deliberately dehumanised blacks. The traffic's enormous profits paid for Britain's industrial revolution, created western financial systems and endowed European cultural institutions. Contemporary Africa's plight and the condition of blacks in the west are blamed on slavery. Europeans should expiate their guilt, runs the demand.

A contrary interpretation is advanced by the vindicators, who argue that slavery occurred in a different moral universe, where all but a lucky few suffered harsh and cruel lives. Africans who sold fellow Africans were equally complicit. Britain seized the high ground with the 1807 Abolition Act, withdrawing from the trade in spite of self-interest and the mores of the time.

This lobby further claims that two centuries is far too long for blacks to maintain a state of victimhood that prevents pragmatic treatment of the real problems that afflict black communities in Africa and elsewhere. An apology is ridiculous, they say. As for reparations: how would they be paid, and to whom?

US President George W. Bush adopted the apologist position when his fulsome retrospective condemnation denounced slavery as "one of the greatest crimes of history", and he paid tribute to the descendants of slaves. "The very people traded into slavery helped to set America free," he declared. His piety glossed over the facts that segregation officially continued until the 1960s, that racism is a clear factor in American life, and that statistics show that blacks are the most underprivileged social group.

With just a few words, Mr. Bush silenced the American "sorry" industry without achieving anything. His words had no impact on social ills that can only be corrected if the ruling elite faces up to uncomfortable truths about our layered and oppressive world—by drafting policy that benefits the poor and invests in society's exploited sections. But the presidential apology made excellent political capital. At the same time, it deflected attention from the real problems that the underclass in the American and African continents suffer today.

This is not to say that past wrongs should be shrugged off. Neither does it justify the vindicators, for the slave trade's dividend is daily manifest in western life. The processing and distribution of tobacco, sugar and cotton produced on plantations resulted in massive investments in European and American ports, quays, warehouses, factories and banks. Cities grew on the back of this trade. Europeans living in the centres of the slave trade—London and Amsterdam—salted away their profits in banks such as Lloyds, which financed slavery. They enjoy visiting the British Museum which started with a collection of 71,000 artifacts collected by Sir Hans Sloane with money made on his wife's Jamaican plantation. Britain's great liberal prime minister, William Gladstone, came from a family whose fortune was made from slavery.

So deeply is modern European life implicated in the trade that a simple "sorry" sounds facetious.

Follow-up action to saying "sorry" is hardly practical. It would demand an impossible balance sheet. How does one assess reparations for a company that began with the slave trade but is now a global corporation employing non-Europeans? For that matter, what about magnificent cultural institutions such as the British Museum? Should concert and theatre halls,

The "Sorry" Movement

Andrew Hawkins [a descendant of Britain's first slave trader, John Hawkins] has turned hand-wringing into performance art. In June the youth theatre director took a guilt trip to Gambia, where he donned a yoke and chain, knelt in front of 16,000 Africans in a football stadium and apologized for what he calls the African holocaust. . . .

The "sorry" movement . . . at the 2000 march for Aboriginal reconciliation has gone global. . . .

Including bonded labourers, there are estimated to be 27 million slaves, and including all categories of trafficked women and children there are estimated to be 100 million slaves. . . .

In response to such shocking statistics, the contrast between practical assistance and self-aggrandising symbolism is striking. While Hawkins is fundraising for another guilt trip, walking in yokes and chains, the Anti-Slavery Society, one of whose earliest members was William Wilberforce, is raising funds to purchase the emancipation of modern slaves and stamp out modern-day slavery.

Rebecca Weisser,
"West Is Master of Slave Trade Guilt,"
The Australian, *December 2, 2006.*
www.theaustralian.news.com.au.

literary trusts and publishing houses funded from slavery's profits all be abolished? Or should hypocrites take over so that an apology makes no difference to enjoying the fruits of inhumanity?

Slavery should be remembered for man's callousness to man. Using it as a political fig leaf to shroud present inequality compounds the wrong. What is required is not a "sorry", but an effort to draw on historical memory to solemnly promise to end the multiplicity of exploitations that still exist.

What is required is not a 'sorry', but an effort to draw on historical memory to solemnly promise to end the multiplicity of exploitations that still exist.

The world wants constructive action, not token gestures.

France Recognizes Past Slavery Crimes Amidst Modern-Day Controversy

Nick Tattersall

In the following article, Reuters reporter Nick Tattersall details the controversy surrounding France's commemoration of the abolition of slavery. While France has recognized past slave trade injustices, little has been done to improve conditions in modern-day France. Many blame the country's colonial past for today's widespread attitudes. Members of France's black community still face racial discrimination and poverty, Tattersall explains, and with shameful evidence that modern-day slavery is thriving, one is left to wonder how much has really changed.

As you read, consider the following questions:

1. At the height of its empire, what portion of colonial Africa did France rule?
2. Where in France do young men from West Africa who are denied visas end up after entering Europe illegally?
3. In what year did France finally abolish slavery?

More than 150 years after the last shackled slave passed through the "door of no return" on Senegal's island of Goree, some Africans wonder how much the colonial balance of power has really changed.

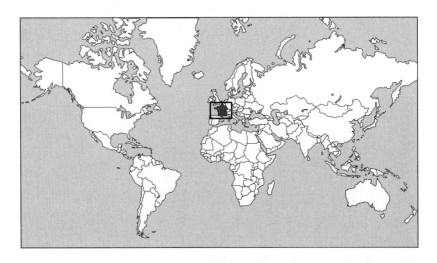

France, its overseas territories and former colonies commemorate the abolition of slavery on Wednesday, a new date chosen by French President Jacques Chirac to mark the adoption of a 2001 law recognising the trade as a crime against humanity.

But for the thousands of young Africans who risk death each year in rickety boats for a life of hard labor on foreign shores, the wrongs of the colonial period have simply given way to a modern-day form of enslavement.

[F]or the thousands of young Africans who risk death each year in rickety boats for a life of hard labor on foreign shores, the wrongs of the colonial period have simply given way to a modern-day form of enslavement.

"We have the impression that France needs the poverty and ignorance of Africa," said Eloi Coly, curator at the Slave House on Senegal's Goree Island, from where an unknown number of slaves were shipped largely to French colonies in the Caribbean between the mid-16th and 19th centuries.

"When France needed to develop after the Second World War it had access to African labor. Now they think African immigrants are the root cause of unemployment and their housing problems," he said, sat in front of the pink stucco building where slaves passed through the "door of no return" as they boarded slave ships.

France ruled over more than a third of Africa at the height of its empire and is still deeply engaged in several former colonies, with military bases dotted around West and Central Africa where French businesses are the major investors.

Critics at home and abroad have blasted France's failure to shake off colonial attitudes, particularly after a law last year urged teachers to stress the "positive role of the French presence overseas."

"We have to be pleased France has recognized slavery as a crime against humanity . . . but there are still a lot of paradoxes and an insufficient knowledge of history," said Alioune Tine, secretary-general of African rights group RADDHO.

"The law on the positive side of colonization profoundly shocked francophone countries in Africa," he told Reuters.

"It seems to be the extreme right influencing immigration policy . . . and modern forms of slavery are alive and well with underpaid workers on the black market."

French Interior Minister Nicolas Sarkozy has drafted a tough law that would make it harder for immigrants to bring relatives to France, force newcomers to take civics lessons and end their automatic right to residence after 10 years.

Who Should Apologize?

With unemployment topping 50 percent in parts of West Africa, young men with no hope of finding work at home are often galled that their former colonial power refuses them visas having reaped the benefit of immigrant labor in the past.

Driven to enter Europe illegally, many end up in the 'banlieues' of Paris and other French cities, soulless suburbs

Colonial Africa, 1914

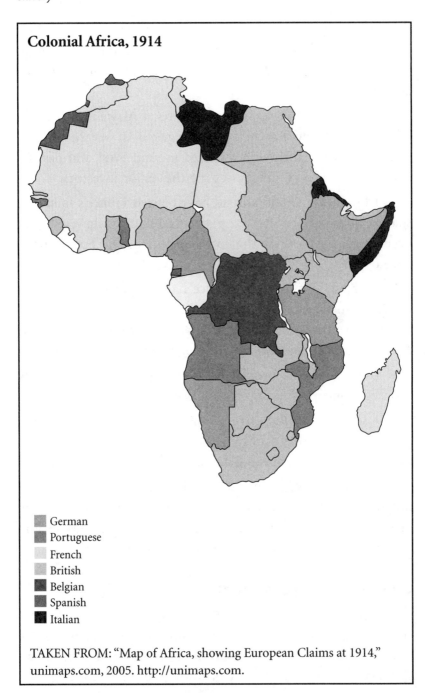

German
Portuguese
French
British
Belgian
Spanish
Italian

TAKEN FROM: "Map of Africa, showing European Claims at 1914," unimaps.com, 2005. http://unimaps.com.

ironically built mainly for immigrant workers welcomed to France after its African colonies gained independence in the 1960s.

Racial segregation in the crime-ridden districts contributed to weeks of rioting last November, with many French-born citizens of African and Arab origin blaming the unrest on what they see as the racist nature of French society.

"There is a form of amnesia and injustice when it comes to all the profit that France has drawn from slavery and from colonization," RADDHO's Tine said.

"If May 10 is to be a meaningful date it has to be a day when these elements are studied and considered," he said.

Estimates suggest between 11 and 12 million slaves were shipped from Africa by European slavers but the question of who should apologize for the trade has proved a thorny one.

France first abolished slavery in 1794 but it was reinstated by Napoleon Bonaparte in 1802, before it was definitively abolished in 1848. Britain will commemorate the 200th anniversary of the abolition of its slave trade next year.

Slavery had long existed in Africa before Europeans turned it into an industry, with slaves captured in battle often sold across the Sahara desert to Arab traders.

"African chiefs were the ones waging war on each other and capturing their own people and selling them," Ugandan President Yoweri Museveni said in an interview when then-U.S. President Bill Clinton toured Africa in 1998.

"If anyone should apologize it should be the African chiefs. We still have those traitors here even today."

Church of England's Apology for Slavery Is a "Good Start"

Ben Fenton

In the following article, journalist Ben Fenton examines the public's reaction to the Church of England's apology for slavery. Some feel that the Church should accompany their words with actions, and that the Church might consider reparations for the families of those who suffered. Fenton provides a historical account of Anglican responsibility in the Caribbean slave trade, noting that slaves of the Church of England can be traced back to as early as 1710.

As you read, consider the following questions:

1. When Christopher Codrington died, what did he leave to the SPG (Society for the Propagation of the Christian Religion in Foreign Parts)?

2. According to the author, why are many institutions as well as the British government apprehensive about apologizing for slavery?

3. Why were slaves on the SPG plantations branded with the word "society" on their chests?

Lisa Codrington knew her ancestors were Anglicans like her and that, almost two centuries ago, they were slaves. But she did not realise until recently that they were slaves of the Church of England.

Ben Fenton, "Church's Slavery Apology 'Is Not Enough,'" *Telegraph*, February 11, 2006. www.telegraph.co.uk. © Copyright of Telegraph Media Group Limited 2006. Reproduced by permission.

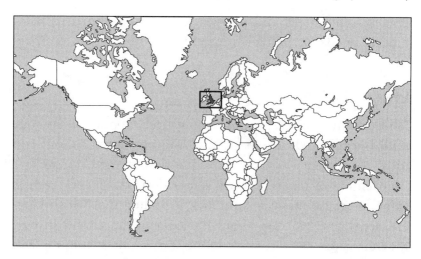

The clue is in her name: Codrington. Slaves of British planters often took the name of their masters and, until 1710, Miss Codrington's forebears lived on the Codrington plantation in Barbados.

After that date, as she discovered for herself a year or two before the apology in this week's [2006] General Synod [the legislative body of the Church] made it clear to the rest of us, the Codrington lands, and the hundreds of slaves on them, became Church property.

The Codrington slaves, men like Devonshire Codrington, born in 1776 and Lisa's many-times great-grandfather, did not become free until 1834, when the Church, like all slave-owners, was forced to release them.

Anglican culpability in the Caribbean slave trade can be traced back at least to 1710, when the planter Christopher Codrington died, leaving his 800-acre Barbados plantations to the Church's newly-established Society for the Propagation of the Christian Religion in Foreign Parts (SPG).

So Miss Codrington and her family are well-placed to comment on the Church's apology. "It's a good start," said the

28-year-old actress and playwright, who was born in Winnipeg, Canada, of Barbadian parents and now works as an actress in Toronto.

What's Next?

"But is that all? I don't know how I feel about the apology until I hear everything about it. Is it involving reparation? Is it involving further work, further education by the Church?"

Mention of reparation will send shivers down ecclesiastical spines, because many institutions, including the British Government, have worried about apologising for slavery in case they are asked to put their money where their mouths are. "The more they do the better they do," she added. "Slavery is not something you can say sorry for and then be done with it."

Miss Codrington has been in Barbados for a month, researching a play about pre-emancipation life, with her mother Hughlene.

Mrs. Codrington left Barbados for Canada in the 1970s, but her daughter has been back several times, fascinated by how much detail she can find about her slave ancestry.

She feels that the Church of England will have got away lightly if nothing more than words come from its bout of self-flagellation. "People have gotten worse [punishments] for doing less," Miss Codrington said. She started to think about her ancestry when a teacher at her drama school asked her to write a monologue "in an accent" and she chose to do it using her mother's native Bajan dialect.

But she has not leapt straight into a quest to lay the blame for her ancestors' sufferings. "I am at the investigative stage right now," she said. "I am the sort of person who likes to understand why things are the way they are.

"I realised that some of these things, like names and faiths, may not have been necessarily matters of choice. They may have been imposed. For me it's more important to figure out

The Codrington Plantations

Christopher Codrington III, died on Good Friday, April 7, 1710. . . . In his will he had left to the Society for the Propagation of the Gospel the estates at Society and Consetts. One of the purposes of the bequest was that there should be maintained a number of professors who should be obliged to teach medicine, surgery and divinity. . . .

For some time the estates were ran by Barbadian planters. . . . Codrington's desire to Christianise the slaves was rejected by the Barbadian plantocracy, who opposed teaching the slaves how to read and write. . . . It was only in 1790 when the anti-slavery movement in England exerted pressure on the Anglican Church and the SPG [Society for the Propagation of the Christian Religion in Foreign Parts] that there was some amelioration in the conditions of the slaves.

"A Historical Overview of Codrington College,"
Codrington College-Codrington.org, 2008. www.codrington.org.

why and try to understand it than to get angry." In north-east London, Miss Codrington's aunt, Ivy Devenish-Scott, 48, an educational consultant, had not heard about the Church's apology until told by *The Daily Telegraph.*

Sins of Omission

Although a Pentecostalist rather than an Anglican, she inclines to be forgiving of the Church of England's past sins towards her family. "I know that the Church, unlike the rest of the plantocracy in Barbados, established the first schools for black children there.

"I am not saying that excuses what they did though, and it would be right for them to provide more now for the families of people who suffered. I don't think a lot of people knew what they did then, and would be appalled, but it seems like an appropriate time to apologise".

"It was not so much the SPG that the Church should be apologizing for as the activities of the individual parsons who kept plantations and slaves for sheer profit."

In Barbados, Woodville Marshall, emeritus professor of history at the University of the West Indies, said the Church's sins over Codrington were those of omission more than commission. "They had professional planters to run the place," he said. "The Church didn't play an active role, because they were more interested in the receipts."

After the plantation was left to the SPG, its slaves were branded on the chest with the word "society", to remind everyone that these were slaves of the Lord. In 1740, 30 years after the Church took over, four out of every 10 slaves bought by the plantation died within three years. "Most people in Barbados are not too troubled by these issues," Prof Marshall said. "It was not so much the SPG that the Church should be apologizing for as the activities of the individual parsons who kept plantations and slaves for sheer profit."

Caribbean Countries Shed Light on the Legacy of Slavery

Orlando Matos

In the following viewpoint, journalist Orlando Matos explores how a new project sponsored by the United Nations Educational, Scientific, and Cultural Organization (UNESCO) is helping to draw attention to the tragic history of slavery while, at the same time, recognizing Africa's important cultural contributions to the countries of the Caribbean, including Aruba, Haiti, Cuba, and the Dominican Republic. The project, Sites of Memory on the Slave Route, will highlight oral expressions, music, dance, and crafts, among other important traditions inherited from African slaves.

As you read, consider the following questions:

1. As explained in the article, what elements were prioritized in the first stage of the project in 2006–2007?

2. Sites of Memory on the Slave Route is a continuation of the Slave Route Project, which got underway in 1994, in what city?

3. According to the article, how many locations did Cuba identify that mark the African heritage on the island?

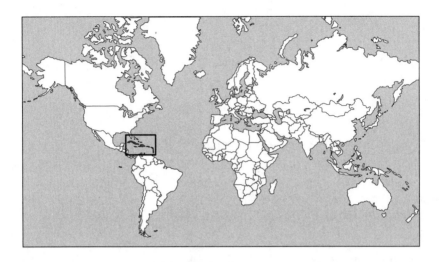

Slavery is inextricably intertwined with the history of the countries of the Caribbean, and a new Sites of Memory on the Slave Route project is focusing on the African influence in Aruba, Haiti, the Dominican Republic and Cuba.

The project, sponsored by UNESCO (United Nations Educational, Scientific, and Cultural Organisation), will put a special emphasis on cultural diversity, development and the cultural legacy of the African diaspora [movement of Africans and their descendants throughout the world].

Frederic Vacheron, a cultural expert in UNESCO's Havana office, told IPS [Inter Press Service] that the originality of the initiative lies in the fact that "besides the physical locations, we have decided to incorporate the immaterial patrimony of these sites."

The dances, songs and traditions inherited from African slaves, as well as the oral and intangible patrimony, will be prioritised in the first stage of the project, in 2006–2007.

The project, launched this month [May 2006] in the Cuban capital, proposes a limit of five sites per country to be developed and eventually turned into cultural tourism destinations. These will be added to the sites already registered on the world heritage list, besides the masterpieces related to the memory of slavery already recognised by UNESCO.

Between 2001 and 2005, the organisation recognised 90 masterpieces, including 17 in Latin America and the Caribbean, representing oral expressions and traditions, music and dance, rituals and mythology, knowledge and practices related to nature and the universe, and traditional crafts.

Vacheron said the project will keep alive the memory of "the tragedy of slavery" while studying the sites as "cultural spaces" and important monuments and reference points of Caribbean culture.

Remembering the African Legacy

The initiative is a continuation of the Slave Route Project which got underway in September 1994 in Ouidah, a city in the West African nation of Benin, "to study closely the profound causes and modalities of the Trans-Atlantic slave trade and to underline the interactions generated by it, in the Americas and the West Indies."

The new project will specifically shed light on the history and effects of slavery in the Caribbean.

Olga Diez, an archaeologist at the University of Barcelona, said "there is still much to be done to recognise this part of African culture, the heritage that slavery brought."

"[T]here is still much to be done to recognise this part of African culture, the heritage that slavery brought."

Diez acknowledged that "there is more awareness than there was 10 years ago," and said she was confident that "another 10 years will not be needed to further raise consciousness" on the influence of the slave trade and slaves in the region.

It is estimated that by the mid-19th century, at least 20 million Africans had become the direct victims of the

Afro-Cuban Identities

In 1860, there were just over 370,000 slaves in Cuba—218,000 were males and 152,000 were females. Over eighty percent were working on the *ingenios* (sugar plantations). Virtually all of these people were African, or of African descent, originating from regions along the West coast of that continent. Most maintained their national identities throughout the period of slavery, and beyond. . . .

Another 185,000 people are estimated to have been brought from other regions of Africa. . . . Free Afro-Cubans were allowed to form *Cabildos,* or mutual aid societies, and these were generally organized according to ethnic origin. These groups served not only as social centers, but also as outlets to express the various cultural traditions that had flowed into the island. They allowed the African way of life many had known before slavery to continue, and shape the religious, artistic and social institutions that define "Cuban" culture today.

"Cuban Society in 1860," The Last Slave Ships,
Mel Fisher Maritime Heritage Society, 2002. www.melfisher.org.

slave trade, a phenomenon that the United Nations recognised in 2001 as a crime against humanity.

"In Aruba, people don't want to remember the problem of slavery," Luc Alofs, curator of the National Museum of History in that country, told IPS. "The current composition of the population, where the European and Amerindian heritage is predominant, fuels that," he added.

Nevertheless, Alofs said that "in recent years there have been changes, and we are working on identifying sites" to keep alive the memory of the African legacy on the island.

In the Dominican Republic, an inventory of sites and places of memory related to the slave trade and slavery is being drawn up, including indigenous settlements along the slave route, because the two groups "coexisted," said Clenis Tavarez, an official at the Museum of Dominican Man in the Dominican Republic.

As Vacheron explained, the project is not limited to the identification of sites, but will also focus on themes that reflect, for example, the link between African and indigenous cultures.

Establishing a Dialogue About Slavery

In Curaçao, which forms part of the slave route but is not included in the Caribbean Regional Slave Route Project, the importance of the influence of slaves has long been recognised. According to Lionel Janga, an expert from that country, "for 30 to 40 years, Curaçao has commemorated everything that has to do with slavery, and we have different heritage sites that we have focused on."

Despite the political and social unrest it has suffered over the past few years, Haiti is also supporting the project. In that nation, "there are no places or towns where the imprints of slavery cannot be found," said Laennec Hurbon, coordinator of the National Haitian Committee for the Slave Route Project.

Cuba has published more than 270 studies and articles on the subject and has identified 735 locations that mark the African heritage on the island, reported Jesús Guanche, a researcher at the Fernando Ortiz Foundation, a nongovernmental Cuban cultural institution.

Guanche called for a deeper study of the "trans-American" slave trade "that inevitably links all of us, in a number of different ways," and enables us "to outline the cultural diversity generated in the shape of inter-American and Caribbean ties."

"The Slave Route is aimed at fomenting intercultural dialogue and pluralism in the broadest sense of the word," and at leaving behind the taboo of talking about slavery, said Vacheron.

"This is an issue that everyone approaches as a cultural question, recognising that it was a tragedy, but that it also left a legacy that we must preserve and revive in future years," the UNESCO official added.

The first results of the project include the publication of inventories of heritage sites in the participating countries, which in the longer term will also be used for other purposes, such as the development of cultural tourism based on the Slave Route and the creation of itineraries that would grant the project a socioeconomic dimension and make it self-sustainable, said Vacheron.

Africans Should Receive Reparations for Slave Trade Crimes

Darcus Howe

In the following viewpoint, Darcus Howe discusses the anti-racism conference held in Durban, South Africa in 2001. He argues that slavery was the beginning of racism, and cites The Marcus Garvey movement, one of the largest anti-racism movements ever executed that demanded reparations for slavery of blacks everywhere. The author insists that the British government, run by then-prime minister Tony Blair, had been turning a blind eye to the possibility of reparations and to the many modern day Africans that were displaced from their homes due to disease and national disasters across the region. Howe is a contributing writer to New Statesman, *broadcaster and social commentator for African rights.*

As you read, consider the following questions:

1. What was The Marcus Garvey movement's slogan? What did it mean?
2. Who is Baroness Amos?
3. What does the author believe Africa, the American South, and other former slave territories need in order to redevelop?

Darcus Howe, "In Durban, a Black Woman Peer Did the White Man's Dirty Work," *New Statesman*, vol. 130, September 10, 2001, p. 22. Copyright © 2001 New Statesman, Ltd. Reproduced by permission.

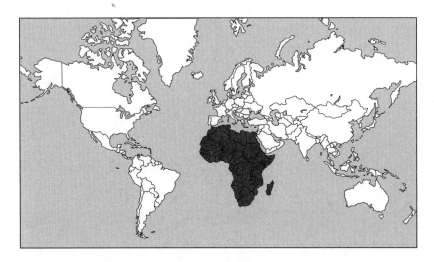

The anti-racism conference held in Durban, South Africa, collapsed in recrimination against Israel, against calls for an apology from Europeans for the Atlantic slave trade, against calls for reparations for one of the most horrible, barbaric, evil, vicious, corrupt moments in the history of humanity.

Nothing else has surpassed slavery and its justification that we who were captured in Africa, and put to work on plantations in America and the Caribbean, were less than human and deserved to be treated that way. It was in this context, backed by the rationale that we were half man/half beast, that racism was born.

Millions of us demand that apology. Those leaders in Africa, the blacks, speak for us. Except the black emissaries of Tony Blair. A hundred years ago, Marcus Garvey led the largest movement in history against racism, against the domination of blacks by whites everywhere. We had made a little progress from the idea of half man/half beast to the new idea that we were simpletons with the underdeveloped minds of children; wholly human, but an inferior species. That still persists in the minds of whites today.

The Marcus Garvey movement demanded reparations for this monumental injustice. "Back to Africa" was the slogan, and millions of blacks warmed to the idea that there should be a wholesale physical shift back to Africa. We saw no future in the Caribbean and none in the United States. But the White House and the leaders of British colonialism needed their negroes and they undermined the movement at every turn. Garvey was imprisoned and died in penury.

Bob Marley immortalised Garvey's manifesto in popular song; he sang it on the night of Zimbabwe's independence. Every single black person knows of that song of freedom, that unbroken link between the plantations of the new world and the continent of Africa.

Simple human respect required that the British government reflect the views of those British citizens who are descended from slaves. Democracy required that we be consulted on at least our general attitude to the idea of an apology and reparations. Nothing of the kind took place. In the eyes of Blair and his Foreign Secretary, Jack Straw, we are still the simpletons, mere children of the white man.

They made up our minds for us. They declared that there would be no apology. Reparations are a non-starter. And whom did they send to Durban to represent the slave masters' views, to do their dirty work for them? One Baroness Amos, an undersecretary of state at the Foreign Office, a woman of Caribbean origin and consequently a descendent of Caribbean slaves. She had to tell all of Africa that she was against apology, against reparations.

The black intellectual elite equates the call for reparations with us being carried away by consumerism. I find this amazing. In the past five years, millions of Africans have been displaced; they have had to walk thousands of miles to find somewhere to live and farm. Disease, national disasters and tribal conflicts have laid waste to rural Africa. The accumulation of capital from African labour and raw materials, the development of technology, have all been transferred to the west. The African elite has collaborated in this from the days of slavery.

Africa's Economic Problems Have Roots in Slavery's Past

For every symptom of Africa's relentless underdevelopment, there is a theory about its root causes. Colonialism, the Cold War, climate change, ethnic warfare, the choking off of technology. . . . But underneath all those, many scholars have long sensed that to answer the two most nagging questions about Africa—How do we fix it? And how did it break?—you have to go much farther back in time. All the way to African slavery. . . .

Could there be a direct, quantifiable link between the African countries most ravaged by slavery and those that are the most underdeveloped today? And if there were such a link, could it be measured?

A young Harvard economist named Nathan Nunn believes there is, and believes he has. In a study [published in the February 2008 *Quarterly Journal of Economics*] sure to stir controversy over the legacy of the African slave trades, Nunn argues that the African countries with the biggest slave exports are by and large the countries with the lowest incomes now. . . .

Nunn argues, if you were an African country that had the most people sold into slavery between 1400 and 1900, then you are likely one of the African countries holding the shortest end of the economic stick today. . . .

Nunn's work also draws attention to the sensitive issue of apologies, reparations, debt relief, and the question of just how much the United States and Europe owe African countries that were at the epicenter of the slave trades.

Francie Latour, "Shackled to the Past,"
The Boston Globe, *April 20, 2008. www.boston.com.*

What we need is a huge transfer of capital, technological know-how and medical expertise back to Africa. And in America, the need is to redevelop the deep south and the inner cities, and to let black talents blossom. This is how reparations would be used, I think, not to allow private black individuals to buy washing machines or DVD players. We need a shift of capital on an epic scale to construct a new world.

The confusion in Durban was a blow, and the clever manipulation of blacks such as Amos was an enormous setback. But the movement for reparations is strong. It will emerge again, with greater strength and conviction.

United States' Payout for Slave Reparations Not Warranted

Peter Flaherty and John Carlisle

Peter Flaherty and John Carlisle argue in the following viewpoint that financial reparations for slavery are unwarranted and would only prompt other ethnic groups in America to seek reparations for similar injustices. International consequences could surface as well, they maintain. Distant descendants of African slaves would qualify for compensation, many now more prosperous than those who would have to pay, while Americans would be punished unfairly since the vast majority of their ancestors immigrated long after slavery was abolished. If financial reparations were made, they reason, reparations-induced resentment would also fuel racial discrimination.

As you read, consider the following questions:

1. When the Chinese immigrated to America in the mid-1800s, how were they discriminated against?
2. What was the population of the free states compared to the free population of the slave-owning states in 1860?
3. Since 1870, roughly how many people have immigrated to the United States?

Peter Flaherty and John Carlisle, "The Case Against Slave Reparations," *The Case Against Slave Reparations*, a monograph published by the National Legal and Policy Center, October 2004, pp. 18–20. www.nlpc.org. Reproduced by permission. The full monograph may be downloaded at http://www.nlpc.org/sites/defualt/files/slavereparations2006.pdf.

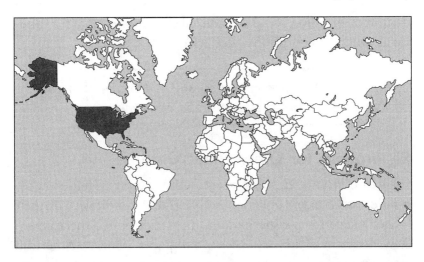

The slave reparations movement is unprecedented in that people are seeking remuneration for the hardships endured by their distant ancestors. Until now, reparations movements always sought compensation for the generations that actually experienced the hardships. To most observers, it defies logic to demand payment for work performed by long-dead generations. But ... this demand must be taken seriously. A notion may be absurd, but if millions of people support it—and stand to profit from it—political momentum for it builds.

A particularly disturbing ramification of compensating descendants of African slaves is the dangerous precedent it would set. It would open up a "Pandora's Box" of other groups seeking reparations for the injustices suffered by their ancestors. Blacks in America, of course, suffered incredible hardships in centuries past. But so did other races. The truth is that, prior to the 20th century, life was exceedingly harsh for the large majority of people. Many of those in positions of power were cruel and unfair—not only to blacks but to people of many races, nationalities and religious creeds. Enlightened ideas of tolerance, fairness, and human rights, which most of us enjoy today, had not yet become widespread throughout the civilized world. Actions that are illegal today—such as slavery, indentured servitude, institutionalized discrimination, and inhumane working conditions—were legal back then.

Blacks in America, of course, suffered incredible hardships in centuries past. But so did other races.

Reparations for Other Ethnic Groups?

Irish immigrants endured severe ethnic discrimination, economic exploitation and deplorable living conditions in their long struggle for prosperity and integration into American society. Ever since the first Irish immigrants came to American shores 300 years ago, they faced enormous resistance to securing social acceptance and civil rights. For example, around 1700 South Carolina instituted a law excluding Irish immigrants. About 15 years later, Maryland passed a similar law, which was ironic in that the colony had been established in part as a haven for Catholics. During later centuries, Irish immigrants were burdened with employment and housing discrimination. Employers and landlords, for example, often posted signs telling Irish immigrants to keep out. A common sign was, "Irish and dogs need not apply."

Many anti-Irish riots occurred in the 1800s in major American cities, in which churches and homes were burned, and Irish immigrants murdered. There was even a major anti-Irish political party, the "Know-Nothing" Party, formed in the 1840s.

In the transatlantic ship crossing, many Irish had to travel in steerage, which was even lower than third class. Living conditions in steerage were inhuman with food often infested with maggots—when food was available at all—and scarce fresh water. Many people died of starvation.

Prior to the Civil War in the South, writer and landscape architect Frederick Law Olmsted observed that Irish immigrants, rather than black slaves, were employed for the most hazardous jobs. For example, while watching black slaves throwing bales into a cargo's ship's hold with Irishmen on the receiving end, Olmsted was told that blacks "are worth too much to be risked here; if the Paddies are knocked overboard . . . nobody loses anything."

The Chinese were another group that faced institutionalized discrimination. When they immigrated to America in the mid-1800s, they faced tremendous anti-Chinese sentiment and discrimination. Laws were passed to restrict them from employment, property ownership, and even from marrying outside their own ethnic group. They also could not live where they wanted, and were confined to certain areas—which are now known as Chinatowns. The Chinese Exclusion Act of 1882 restricted them from immigrating to America. Their basic rights were not fully restored until the 1960s.

Opening "Pandora's Box"

The histories of numerous other ethnic groups are filled with similar stories. Such groups include Hispanic Americans, Italian Americans, Polish Americans, German Americans, Russian Americans, Portuguese Americans, Scottish Americans, Armenian Americans, Greek Americans, Filipino Americans, and many more.

If slave reparations were ever enacted, it would not at all be far-fetched to expect other ethnic groups to demand similar types of reparations for past bouts of discrimination. Indeed, claims for Chinese American reparations may not be far behind. Under California's state law requiring insurance companies to file disclosures of past links to slavery, the California Insurance Department found evidence that Manhattan Life provided an insurance policy to shippers for 700 Chinese laborers on a voyage from China in 1854.

Not only would the prospect of slave reparations open a "Pandora's Box" of other ethnic groups demanding money for historical injustices, but groups would no doubt demand even more reparations. There would be complaints that initial reparations did not go far enough. If, for example, the U.S. government paid out a billion dollars in reparations to African Americans, activists would point out that the total value of slaves' work, with interest, was much higher than that—in the hundreds of billions or trillions of dollars. The potential for "reparations inflation" is infinite.

Moreover, if reparations were paid, activists would see that poverty still exists among blacks, and that real or imagined incidents of racial discrimination continue to occur. Blacks would perceive that nothing much had changed; and . . . reparations-induced resentment toward blacks by non-blacks, in fact, would increase. Blacks would claim that the solution is even more reparations. And the vicious cycle would continue.

Suing Today for Yesterday's Working Conditions

Based on slave reparation advocates' logic, those whose ancestors toiled in factories in the 19th and early 20th centuries— underpaid and in hellish working conditions—should be entitled to compensation. At that time, there were not the same types of employment laws that exist now. Just as blacks are demanding to be compensated for slavery, an illegal practice today but legal in the 19th century, whites could use the same justification to demand compensation for working conditions that are now illegal but were legal in the early 20th century.

Could this be on the agenda of labor unions if the slave reparations advocates succeed? They could sue for billions, based on this line of reasoning. Slavery, to be sure, was an abomination, but so was child labor, disease-ridden factories, indentured servitude and other legalized forms of labor of that era. Were such practices widespread in the 20th or 21st centuries, after laws had been passed outlawing them, the victims could sue for tremendous damages.

"But my ancestors came to America in 1900. Shut up and write the check White Boy!" cartoon by Brian Fairrington. Copyright © 2002 Brian Fairrington and Political Cartoons.com.

And what about descendants of the original colonists from England? Adopting the mentality of slave reparations advocates, even they could demand reparations. . . . [M]any of the original inhabitants from Europe came as white slaves. According to historian John Van Der Zee, half of the original American colonists came here not of their own free will, but either as indentured servants (which is slavery, albeit not for life), or as slaves for life.

International Repercussions

If the reparations advocates succeed, there could be international repercussions as well. Latin Americans could start demanding that the governments of Spain and Portugal compensate them for the death and devastation they suffered at the hands of the Conquistadors in the 16th century.

Inspired by the slave reparations controversy brewing in the United States, African nations are already demanding country-to-country reparations. At the hyperbolic-named "U.N. [United Nations] World Conference Against Racism, Racial Discrimination, Xenophobia, and Related Intolerance" that took place in Durban, South Africa in 2001, one of the biggest issues was African nations' demand that Europe and America apologize and compensate for the slave trade. . . .

Of course, even if Western nations took the unlikely step of giving Africa billions of dollars in slave reparations, it would do nothing to resolve the endemic poverty, tyranny and civil war plaguing the continent. Ironically, the African delegates to the U.N. conference were reluctant to discuss the very real problem of modern-day slavery in Africa. . . . This is to say nothing of Africans' own heavy involvement in slave trading during earlier centuries; in most cases, . . . it was Africans themselves who sold slaves to the Europeans and Americans.

[E]ven if Western nations took the unlikely step of giving Africa billions of dollars in slave reparations, it would do nothing to resolve the endemic poverty, tyranny and civil war plaguing the continent.

Nonvictims Punishing the Innocent

The notion of paying recompense for what one's distant ancestor did a century and a half ago is nonsensical. Yet that is what advocates of slave reparations are demanding. Equally disturbing, the people who would receive the money are not the victims, but the great-great-great grandchildren of the victims, many of whom are much more prosperous than those who would have to pay.

But the absurdity of reparations goes much beyond that. First, only a tiny minority of Americans today has an ancestor who was a slave owner. Prior to and during the Civil War, the great majority of the population was located in the northern states where slavery was outlawed. In 1860, the population of the free states totaled about 19.5 million; the free population of the slave-owning states was 7.5 million. This means that among Americans today who had ancestors living in the United States during the slavery era, most of those ancestors lived in the non-slave owning northern states. In fact, many of those northerners were abolitionists and detested the institution of slavery.

As for the small number of Americans alive today who had ancestors living in the antebellum South, chances are those ancestors were not slave owners. Only one out of four southern whites owned slaves. Thus, only a very small percentage of contemporary Americans have direct ancestors who were slave owners. Other Americans perhaps have distant uncles or cousins who were slave owners. If reparations were mandated, this would be a case of paying recompense for an act carried out by a distant cousin of a long-deceased direct ancestor.

[T]he vast majority of Americans' ancestors did not even live in the United States when slavery was legal. They immigrated here after slavery was abolished.

Most Americans Immigrated After Slavery Ended

Even more significant is that the vast majority of Americans' ancestors did not even live in the United States when slavery was legal. They immigrated here after slavery was abolished. . . . There were 9.5 million people in the U.S. in 1820. Between 1820 and 1860, when slavery existed, about 5 million people immigrated to the U.S., the large majority going to the non-slave owning states and territories. . . .

[T]he great waves of immigration took place after the Civil War ended in 1865, particularly around 1900, as well as the most recent decade. Since 1870, more than 51 million people have immigrated to the United States.

Everyone can agree that the more than 45 million Americans of Latin American and Asian descent are completely absolved of any complicity with U.S. slavery, since almost all of their ancestors immigrated to the U.S. long after slavery ended, most of them in recent decades. And of the very few people of Latin American or Asian origin who were U.S. citizens during the slavery era, it is safe to say that very few of them were slave owners.

Japan's Reparation Fund for Former Sex Slaves Is Met with Resentment

Norimitsu Onishi

In the following viewpoint, New York Times *correspondent Norimitsu Onishi investigates how Japan's attempt to compensate victims of wartime sexual slavery was met with opposition. According to Onishi, the countries Japan hoped to reconcile with did not respond favorably, and by the time the fund was closed in 2007, only a fraction of victims were willing to accept compensation. Many refused to accept the money because the fund was not a government fund, Onishi contends, while others who accepted compensation were secretive, afraid of being criticized.*

As you read, consider the following questions:

1. According to Onishi, why did Japan's decision to set up the Asian Women's Fund as a private fund provoke anger?

2. How much money did the Japanese government provide in "welfare services"?

3. Where was opposition to the fund the strongest, according to the Onishi?

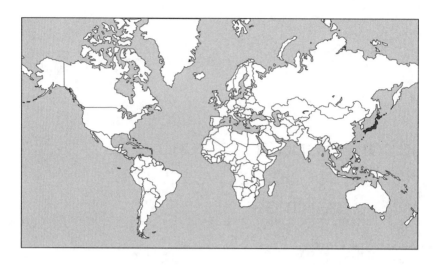

Facing calls to compensate the aging victims of its wartime sexual slavery, Japan set up the Asian Women's Fund in 1995. It was a significant concession from Japan, which has always asserted that postwar treaties absolved it of all individual claims from World War II.

But the fund only fueled anger in the very countries with which Japan had sought reconciliation.

By the time it closed as scheduled last month, only a fraction of the former sex slaves had accepted its money. Two Asian governments even offered money to discourage more women from taking Japan's.

Critics inside and outside Japan complained about the Japanese government's decision to set up the fund as a private one, making clear that the "atonement" payments came from citizens. They saw this as another tortured attempt by Tokyo to avoid taking full responsibility for one of the ugliest aspects of the war.

"It was not directly from the Japanese government; that is why I did not accept it," said Ellen van der Ploeg, 84, a Dutchwoman who was taken from a prisoner of war camp in Indonesia and forced to work in a Japanese military brothel for three months in 1944. "If you have made mistakes in life, you must have the courage to say, 'I'm sorry, please forgive me.' But the Japanese government to this day has never taken full responsibility."

"If this were a pure government fund, I could have accepted it," Ms. van der Ploeg said in a telephone interview from Houten, the Netherlands. "Why should I accept money from private Japanese people? They were also victims during the war."

The Japanese government has held up the fund as one way it has tried to redress a past wrong, even as, in Washington, the House of Representatives is considering a resolution that would call on Japan's government to unequivocally acknowledge its role in the wartime sexual slavery, and apologize for it.

Of those former sex slaves—known euphemistically here as comfort women—who accepted money from the fund, most did so secretly to avoid criticism. Supporters of the women in the four places where women were compensated individually—South Korea, Taiwan, the Philippines and the Netherlands—became deeply divided over whether to accept the money.

Of those former sex slaves—known euphemistically here as comfort women—who accepted money from the fund, most did so secretly to avoid criticism.

Even those who favored accepting the money said the fund reflected the absence of moral clarity in Japan, an opinion that was reinforced in March, when Prime Minister Shinzo Abe denied the Japanese military's role in coercing women into sexual slavery.

"I believed the Japanese government should take direct legal responsibility, but I respected the wishes of the women who wanted to accept the money," said Marguerite Hamer, the head of a private Dutch organization, the Project Implementation Committee in the Netherlands, through which 79 women have received compensation from the Asian Women's Fund. "They are old, and they had such hard lives."

"I was furious and astounded by Abe's denial," Ms. Hamer added. "It was really awful for the women. Four of them called me and said, 'How could this happen again? How could they do this to me again?'"

About $4.8 million was raised for the fund from private contributions. From that sum, 285 women in South Korea, Taiwan and the Philippines received almost $17,000 each, along with a letter of apology from the Japanese prime minister.

About $4.8 million was raised for the fund from private contributions.

The Japanese government stressed that the "atonement money" did not come from the government, in keeping with its position that postwar treaties cleared it of such claims. It also feared, experts said, that making any exceptions would leave it vulnerable to lawsuits from other victims of Japanese militarism.

The government provided $6.3 million in "welfare services" to the 285 women, as well as the 79 in the Netherlands. This money was also part of the Asian Women's Fund. In reality, though, the women were free to use this government money however they wished. There was little practical difference, but a big symbolic one, between atonement and welfare.

An Open Wound

In a highly unusual move, the lower house of the Dutch parliament passed a motion unanimously Tuesday [November 20, 2007], urging Japan to financially compensate the women forced into sex slavery during World War II. . . .

Van Baalen [Hans, Dutch Lawmaker] believes that Japan's denial of the past war crimes has hurt its relations with the Netherlands, with which Japan is to celebrate 400 years of trade ties in 2009.

Failure to recognize the past and take responsibility for its war crimes prevent Japan from mending relations with the countries it invaded in the 1940s, he said.

"The wound won't heal unless Japan shows sincere remorse for its war atrocities," he said, adding that paying a justifiable material compensation would help demonstrate Japan's sincerity.

Sun Yunlong,
"Dutch Parliament Demands Japanese
Compensation for 'Comfort Women,'" Xinhuanet,
November 21, 2007. http://news.xinhuanet.com.

"The Japanese government has presented this fund to deceive our survivors and the international community," said Nelia Sancho, a leading supporter of the women in the Philippines.

As a result of the hairsplitting, the governments of Taiwan and South Korea, two former Japanese colonies, rejected both payment programs of the Asian Women's Fund and created their own. Former sex slaves there were pressed to reject the Japanese money, though supporters acknowledge that some secretly accepted both.

Haruki Wada, the executive director of the Asian Women's Fund and a historian at the University of Tokyo, defended the program, noting that it was Japan's first attempt since the end of World War II to compensate its war victims individually.

He acknowledged that the nature of the payments was sometimes confusing.

"The Dutch took it as compensation, but for the Japanese government, it wasn't compensation," Mr. Wada said. "In theory, the payments were for the costs of the welfare services. It was a quintessentially Japanese way of doing things."

He added, "It doesn't matter if there's criticism that the fund was inadequate or that Japan should have done more. But to tell the victims that they can't take this money only made them suffer."

Mr. Wada said fund officials were unable to operate and reach survivors in other countries, including China, North Korea, Malaysia, Myanmar and East Timor.

Because of the official opposition in South Korea and Taiwan, officials associated with the Japanese fund often had to contact former sex slaves outside official channels.

Wu Huiling, an official at the Taipei Women's Rescue Foundation—the private organization that has been entrusted by the Taiwanese government to offer services to former sex slaves—said fund officials sometimes came knocking, unannounced, at the women's homes.

"The grandmas were surprised," Ms. Wu said. "At first, they thought the strangers were con men, but they were only men from the Asian Women's Fund offering them money."

Because of the delicateness of the issue, officials at the Japanese fund have refused to break down the 285 recipients by nationality.

"This fund is closing without our being able to even announce how many accepted the fund in South Korea and Taiwan," Mr. Wada said.

Indeed, the opposition was fiercest in South Korea.

In a shelter for former sex slaves outside Seoul, Yi Ok-seon, 80, said the fund was an attempt by the Japanese government "to shut the mouths of the comfort women."

Between 1942 and 1945, starting at age 16, another Korean woman, Lee Yong-nyeo, 81, was forced to work in a military brothel in Burma, now Myanmar. She was one of the few in South Korea to admit taking money from the fund.

"I lived in someone else's house since I was 8, and I wanted to buy land," said Mrs. Lee, in an interview inside the new house she bought with money from the fund.

"I resisted for many years," she added. "But I didn't know whether I would ever get anything, so when the Japanese called a few years ago and said this might be the last chance, I decided to accept it."

In the Philippines, the government offered no domestic assistance to the women and avoided criticizing Japan, by far its largest donor. "The Filipino government is so dependent on Japanese aid that it cannot rock the boat," said Ricardo Trota Jose, a historian of Philippine-Japanese relations at the University of the Philippines.

Periodical Bibliography

The following articles have been selected to supplement the diverse views presented in this chapter.

Jamila Ahmadu   "Do You Remember the Days of Slavery?" *Daily Trust*, December 25, 2007. www.dailytrust.com.

Te-Ping Chen   "Tracing Slavery's Past," *The Nation*, March 14, 2008. www.thenation.com.

Darryl Fears   "Slavery Apology: A Sincere Step or Mere Politics?" *Washington Post*, August 2, 2008. www.washingtonpost.com.

Paul Gleason   "Slavery's Sway," *Harvard Magazine*, November–December 2008. http://harvardmagazine.com.

Vanessa E. Jones   "Neglected," *The Boston Globe*, June 24, 2008. www.bostonglobe.com.

Ban Ki-moon   "Past Injustices Should Spur Battle Against Modern Forms of Slavery," UN News Centre, March 25, 2008. www.un.org.

Justin McCurry   "Japan Avoids Full Apology for War Sex Slavery," Guardian News, March 27, 2007. www.guardian.co.uk.

Walter Olson   "Slavery Reparations: What Happened?" *Los Angeles Times*, October 31, 2008. www.latimes.com.

Gary Pieters   "Slavery's Long Destructive Legacy," *Toronto Star*, March 24, 2007. www.thestar.com.

Christine Vestal   "States Lead Slavery Apology Movement," Stateline.org. April 4, 2008. www.stateline.org.

GLOBALVIEWPOINTS

CHAPTER 2

Slavery in Modern Times

Human Trafficking and Exploitation Today: An Overview

U.S. Department of State

In the following viewpoint, the U.S. Department of State defines human trafficking as a number of different aspects of the commercial sex or recruitment of children into labor or soldiering industry. "The common denominator of trafficking scenarios," the report says, "is the use of force, fraud, or coercion to exploit a person for profit." According to a 2006 U.S. annual report, approximately 800,000 persons were trafficked that year, and among them are women and children that have either been sold or taken from their families and prostituted in some way into trafficking.

As you read, consider the following questions:

1. According to the United Nations, how many people are forced labor, bonded labor, forced child labor, and sexual servitude at any given time?

2. By both the United Nations and U.S. definitions of trafficking, does the victim need to be moved across borders in order to be considered a trafficked person? What is the common denominator among all definitions of human trafficking?

"Trafficking in Persons Report," Office of the Under Secretary for Democracy and Global Affairs and Bureau of Public Affairs, U.S. Department of State, June 2008.

3. What are some of the consequences for minors that have been victims commercial sex trafficking?

Human Trafficking Defined

The TVPA [Trafficking Victims Protection Act of 2000] defines "severe forms of trafficking" as:

a. sex trafficking in which a commercial sex act is induced by force, fraud, or coercion, or in which the person induced to perform such an act has not attained 18 years of age; or

b. the recruitment, harboring, transportation, provision, or obtaining of a person for labor or services, through the use of force, fraud, or coercion for the purpose of subjection to involuntary servitude, peonage, debt bondage, or slavery.

A victim need not be physically transported from one location to another in order for the crime to fall within these definitions.

The Scope and Nature of Modern-Day Slavery

The common denominator of trafficking scenarios is the use of force, fraud, or coercion to exploit a person for profit. A victim can be subjected to labor exploitation, sexual exploitation, or both. Labor exploitation includes traditional chattel slavery, forced labor, and debt bondage. Sexual exploitation typically includes abuse within the commercial sex industry. In other cases, victims are exploited in private homes by individuals who often demand sex as well as work. The use of force or coercion can be direct and violent or psychological.

A wide range of estimates exists on the scope and magnitude of modern-day slavery. The International Labor Organization (ILO)—the United Nations agency charged with addressing labor standards, employment, and social protection issues—estimates that there are 12.3 million people in forced labor, bonded labor, forced child labor, and sexual servitude at any given time; other estimates range from 4 million to 27 million.

Annually, according to U.S. Government sponsored research completed in 2006, approximately 800,000 people are trafficked across national borders, which does not include millions trafficked within their own countries. Approximately 80 percent of transnational victims are women and girls and up to 50 percent are minors. The majority of transnational victims are females trafficked into commercial sexual exploitation. These numbers do not include millions of female and male victims around the world who are trafficked within their own national borders—the majority for forced or bonded labor.

Human traffickers prey on the vulnerable. Their targets are often children and young women, and their ploys are creative and ruthless, designed to trick, coerce, and win the confidence of potential victims. Very often these ruses involve promises of a better life through employment, educational opportunities, or marriage.

The nationalities of trafficked people are as diverse as the world's cultures. Some leave developing countries, seeking to improve their lives through low-skilled jobs in more prosperous countries. Others fall victim to forced or bonded labor in their own countries. Women, eager for a better future, are susceptible to promises of jobs abroad as babysitters, housekeepers, waitresses, or models—jobs that traffickers turn into the nightmare of forced prostitution without exit. Some families give children to adults, often relatives, who promise education and opportunity—but sell the children into exploitative situations for money. But poverty alone does not explain this tragedy, which is driven by fraudulent recruiters, employers, and corrupt officials who seek to reap unlawful profits from others' desperation. . . .

Forced Labor and Sexual Servitude: The Varying Forms of Human Trafficking

The hidden nature of trafficking in persons prevents a precise count of the number of victims around the world, but available research indicates that, when trafficking within a country's borders is included in the count, more people fall victim to labor forms of trafficking than sex trafficking. Although labor trafficking and sex trafficking are usually analyzed as separate trafficking in persons issues, victims of both forms of trafficking often share a common denominator: their trafficking ordeal started with a migration in search of economic alternatives.

The theme of migration is often heard in reporting on trafficking in persons and indeed the movement of victims is a common trait in many trafficking crimes. Yet servitude can also occur without the movement of a person. In analyzing trafficking in persons issues and designing effective responses, the focus should be on the exploitation and control of a person through force, fraud, or coercion – not on the movement of that person.

Neither the international definition of trafficking in persons, as defined in the 2000 UN Protocol to Prevent, Suppress, and Punish Trafficking in Persons, Especially Women and Children, nor the U.S. definition of severe forms of trafficking in persons, as defined in federal law, requires the movement of the victim. Movement is not necessary, as any person who is recruited, harbored, provided, or obtained through force, fraud, or coercion for the purpose of subjecting that person to involuntary servitude, forced labor, or commercial sex qualifies as a trafficking victim.

Forced Labor

Most instances of forced labor occur as unscrupulous employers take advantage of gaps in law enforcement to exploit vulnerable workers. These workers are made more vulnerable to forced labor practices because of unemployment, poverty, crime, discrimination, corruption, political conflict, and cultural acceptance of the practice. Immigrants are particularly vulnerable, but individuals are also forced into labor in their own countries. Female victims of forced or bonded labor, especially women and girls in domestic servitude, are often sexually exploited as well.

Forced labor is a form of human trafficking that can be harder to identify and estimate than sex trafficking. It may not involve the same criminal networks profiting from transnational sex trafficking, but may instead involve individuals who subject anywhere from one to hundreds of workers to involuntary servitude, perhaps through forced or coerced household work or work at a factory.

Bonded Labor

One form of force or coercion is the use of a bond, or debt, to keep a person under subjugation. This is referred to in law and policy as "bonded labor" or "debt bondage." It is criminalized under U.S. law and included as a form of exploitation related to trafficking in the UN TIP Protocol. Many workers around the world fall victim to debt bondage when traffickers or recruiters unlawfully exploit an initial debt the worker assumed as part of the terms of employment, or when workers inherit debt in more traditional systems of bonded labor. Traditional bonded labor in South Asia enslaves huge numbers of people from generation to generation.

Debt Bondage and Involuntary Servitude Among Migrant Laborers

The vulnerability of migrant laborers to trafficking schemes is especially disturbing because this population is so sizeable in some regions. Three potential contributors can be discerned: 1) Abuse of contracts; 2) Inadequate local laws governing the recruitment and employment of migrant laborers; and 3) The intentional imposition of exploitative and often illegal costs and debts on these laborers in the source country or state, often with the complicity and/or support of labor agencies and employers in the destination country or state.

Some abuses of contracts and hazardous conditions of employment do not in themselves constitute involuntary servitude, though use or threat of physical force or restraint to compel a worker to enter into or continue labor or service may convert a situation into one of forced labor. Costs imposed on laborers for the "privilege" of working abroad can place laborers in a situation highly vulnerable to debt bondage. However, these costs alone do not constitute debt bondage or involuntary servitude. When combined with exploitation by unscrupulous labor agents or employers in the destination country, these costs or debts, when excessive, can become a form of debt bondage.

Involuntary Domestic Servitude

Domestic workers may be trapped in servitude through the use of force or coercion, such as physical (including sexual) or emotional abuse. Children are particularly vulnerable. Domestic servitude is particularly difficult to detect because it occurs in private homes, which are often unregulated by public authorities. For example, there is great demand in some wealthier countries of Asia and the Middle East for domestic servants who sometimes fall victim to conditions of involuntary servitude.

Forced Child Labor

Most international organizations and national laws recognize that children may legally engage in light work. In contrast, the worst forms of child labor are being targeted for eradication by nations across the globe. The sale and trafficking of children and their entrapment in bonded and forced labor are clearly among the worst forms of child labor. Any child who is subject to involuntary servitude, debt bondage, peonage, or slavery through the use of force, fraud, or coercion is a victim of trafficking in persons regardless of the location of that exploitation.

Child Soldiers

Child soldiering is a unique and severe manifestation of trafficking in persons that involves the unlawful recruitment of children through force, fraud, or coercion to be exploited for their labor or to be abused as sex slaves in conflict areas. Such unlawful practices may be perpetrated by government forces, paramilitary organizations, or rebel groups. UNICEF estimates that more than 300,000 children under 18 are currently being exploited in more than 30 armed conflicts worldwide. While the majority of child soldiers are between the ages of 15 and 18, some are as young as 7 or 8 years of age.

Many children are abducted to be used as combatants. Others are made unlawfully to serve as porters, cooks, guards, servants, messengers, or spies. Many young girls are forced to marry or have sex with male combatants and are at high risk of unwanted pregnancies. Male and female child soldiers are often sexually abused and are at high risk of contracting sexually transmitted diseases.

Some children have been forced to commit atrocities against their families and communities. Child soldiers are often killed or wounded, with survivors often suffering multiple traumas and psychological scarring. Their personal development is often irreparably damaged. Returning child soldiers are often rejected by their home communities.

Child soldiers are a global phenomenon. The problem is most critical in Africa and Asia, but armed groups in the Americas and the Middle East also unlawfully use children in conflict areas. All nations must work together with interna-

Human Trafficking for Forced Labor

Rajila, age 30, left her home in India to work in Saudi Arabia based on promises of a good salary and free housing from a company that supplies laborers for hospitals. But what seemed like a dream opportunity turned out to be a nightmare. Rajila, together with other foreign women, was forced to work 12-hour shifts, six days a week. She was never paid. The "free" housing was excruciatingly confining, and, when the women returned from work, they were locked in their rooms. . . . Rajila left Saudi Arabia taking with her no accumulated salary from three and a half years of uninterrupted work.

Trafficking in persons is modern-day slavery. Every year, approximately 800,000 people are trafficked across international borders; millions more are enslaved in their own countries. The common denominator in all trafficking scenarios is the use of force, fraud or coercion to exploit a person for commercial sex or for the purpose of subjecting a victim to involuntary servitude, debt bondage, or forced labor. The use of force or coercion can be direct and violent, or psychological.

Most instances of forced labor occur as unscrupulous recruiters and employers take advantage of gaps in law enforcement to exploit vulnerable workers. . . .

Victims of trafficking for forced labor are modern-day slaves. They experience permanent physical and psychological harm, isolation from their families and communities, reduced opportunities for personal development, and restricted movement. . . . Child victims are denied access to education, which reinforces the cycle of illiteracy and poverty that facilitates their exploitation.

*United States Department of State,
"Fact Sheet: The Facts About Human Trafficking for Forced Labor,"
Office to Monitor and Combat Trafficking in Persons,
June 3, 2008. www.state.gov.*

tional organizations and NGOs [Non-Government Organizations] to take urgent action to disarm, demobilize, and reintegrate child soldiers.

Sex Trafficking and Prostitution

Sex trafficking comprises a significant portion of overall trafficking and the majority of transnational modern-day slavery. Sex trafficking would not exist without the demand for commercial sex flourishing around the world. The U.S. Government adopted a strong position against prostitution in a December 2002 policy decision, which notes that prostitution is inherently harmful and dehumanizing, and fuels trafficking in persons. Turning people into dehumanized commodities creates an enabling environment for human trafficking.

Children Exploited for Commercial Sex

Each year, more than two million children are exploited in the global commercial sex trade. Many of these children are trapped in prostitution. The commercial sexual exploitation of children is trafficking, regardless of circumstances. International covenants and protocols obligate criminalization of the commercial sexual exploitation of children. The use of children in the commercial sex trade is prohibited under both U.S. law and the U.N. TIP Protocol. There can be no exceptions, no cultural or socio-economic rationalizations that prevent the rescue of children from sexual servitude. Terms such as "child sex worker" are unacceptable because they falsely sanitize the brutality of this exploitation.

Child Sex Tourism

Child sex tourism (CST) involves people who travel from their own country—often a country where child sexual exploitation is illegal or culturally abhorrent—to another country where they engage in commercial sex acts with children. CST is a shameful assault on the dignity of children and a form of violent child abuse. The commercial sexual exploitation of children has devastating consequences for minors, which may include long-lasting physical and psychological trauma, disease (including HIV/AIDS), drug addiction, unwanted pregnancy, malnutrition, social ostracism, and possibly death. Tourists engaging in CST often travel to developing countries looking for anonymity and the availability of children in prostitution. The crime is typically fueled by weak law enforcement, corruption, the Internet, ease of travel, and poverty. Sex offenders come from all socio-economic backgrounds and may in some cases hold positions of trust. Cases of child sex tourism involving U.S. citizens have included a pediatrician, a retired Army sergeant, a dentist, and a university professor. Child pornography is frequently involved in these cases, and drugs may also be used to solicit or control the minors.

Burmese Migrant Workers in Malaysia Are at the Mercy of International Trafficking Gangs

Luisetta Mudie

In Malaysia, Burmese migrant workers are trapped in a "human rights no-man's land," treated as disposable commodities after losing their legal status—their passports often kept by employers. After being forced into covert jails or deportation camps, they fall victim to trafficking gangs who sell them back and forth with cooperation from Malaysian and Thai immigration officials. The following article, written by Luisetta Mudie, with original reporting in Burmese by Kyaw Min Htun, explores this deplorable trade in humans and investigates why Malaysia needs to make drastic improvements in the legal protection of foreign migrant workers' rights.

As you read, consider the following questions:

1. According to the article, roughly how many illegal foreign workers are in Malaysia?

2. What is the primary responsibility of RELA (Ikatan Relawan Rakyat Malaysia, or Volunteers of the Malaysian People)?

3. Of the active asylum cases pending in Malaysia in 2006, what percentage of those persons were Burmese?

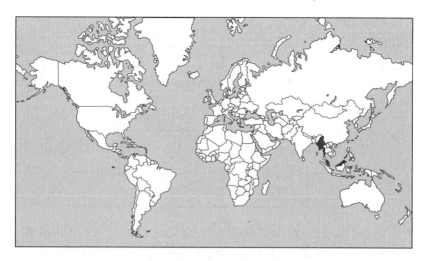

Burmese migrant workers in Malaysia live at the mercy of international human-trafficking gangs who sell them back and forth as slave labor with the full knowledge of Malaysian and Thai immigration officials, RFA's [Radio Free Asia] Burmese service reports.

Thousands and perhaps hundreds of thousands of Burmese find themselves stuck in a human rights no-man's land after losing their legal status, often because employers withhold passports or refuse to pay their return airfares.

"To tell the truth, we Burmese aren't even as valuable as dogs in this country," Burmese laborer Ko Chit Aye said. "Most of the time, Burmese people work in construction and on farms, but most employers cheat them. Most of them ask people to work without paying them money. Many of them don't pay."

In the murky world inhabited by thousands of Burmese in relatively prosperous Malaysia, there is scant protection for human rights as Malaysia doesn't recognize key international agreements on the protection of refugees and foreign nationals. Nor does it apply to foreign migrants the same rights protections offered to Malaysian citizens.

Several secret jails or deportation camps exist around the country to hold foreign nationals found without papers. From there, officials take them to the Thai border, where trafficking gangs have close ties to Malaysian officials and have been tipped off to their arrival.

[T]here is scant protection for human rights as Malaysia doesn't recognize key international agreements on the protection of refugees and foreign nationals.

"Almost all agents, one way or the other, are politically connected," said Malaysian legislator Kula Segaram, who is campaigning to boost legal protection of foreign migrant workers' rights.

"It's Big Business"

"They are all in the human-trafficking business. It's big business. Big money," said Segaram, who confirmed reports throughout Malaysia from stranded and trafficked Burmese migrants who say they are hounded either by immigration militia or by human-trafficking gangs with connections at every level of Malaysian society.

"It's because these agents and brokers are connected to the authorities in one way or another. They are all involved in the human-trafficking business. This is a very big business that is bringing in a lot of money. I'm talking about U.S. $500 per person. In Malaysia, there are 2 million illegal foreign workers. You can just calculate the income," Segaram said.

Typically, a Burmese worker is recruited by agents at home with promises of a lucrative job and matched with an employer, who then withholds his or her passport.

Often, when their contract ends, the employer refuses to pay the worker's return airfare, as employers are legally obliged to do. Instead, the Burmese worker is turned loose without documentation to live on the run, or is taken to a detention center to await deportation.

Right to Raid Homes, Make Arrests

A spokeswoman for the Malaysian human rights group Suaram said the government was making its own problems.

"The refugee problems in Malaysia are caused by Malaysian immigration. They are the main people who create these problems, and they don't solve them," the spokeswoman told reporter Kyaw Min Htun. "It's because they've given the RELA militia group, which doesn't deserve that much power, a lot of power and the right to raid homes and arrest people. That's why the refugees are victimized," she said.

RELA denotes the Ikatan Relawan Rakyat Malaysia, or Volunteers of the Malaysian People, a civil corps formed by the government whose primary responsibility is verifying travel documents and immigration permits held by foreigners.

RELA has authority to raid suspect premises and interrogate or detain people found without the proper documents. The U.S. State Department has described RELA as a corps of 440,000 citizens under the Home Affairs Ministry that accompanies police and immigration officials on raids.

"Following repeated media reports of alleged abusive behavior and inappropriate language by RELA members during raids, in February [2006] the Home Affairs Ministry stated that only a small minority of RELA members would be allowed to participate in operations against illegal migrants and that RELA officers remained prohibited from body searching a suspect," it said.

While Malaysian immigration law provides for six months in prison and up to six strokes of the cane for immigration violations, "delays in processing travel documents led to the detention of many illegal immigrants in camps for more than a year," the State Department said in its most recent report on human rights around the world.

Disposable Slaves

Slaves of the past were worth stealing and worth chasing down if they escaped. Today slaves cost so little that it is not worth the hassle of securing permanent, "legal" ownership. Slaves are disposable. . . .

The key differences between old and new forms of slavery break down like this:

Old Slavery	New Slavery
Legal ownership asserted	Legal ownership avoided
High purchase cost	Very low purchase cost
Low profits	Very high profits
Shortage of potential slaves	Glut of potential slaves
Long-term relationships	Short-term relationship
Slaves maintained	Slaves disposable
Ethnic differences important	Ethnic differences less important

Kevin Bales,
"The New Slavery," Disposable People,
Berkeley and Los Angeles: University of California Press, Ltd., 2004.

International rights groups say the Malaysian government has done little to prevent the trade in human beings.

Calls to the Malaysian immigration department in Kuala Lumpur met with constant deferral of requests for interviews with officials in charge of illegal immigration.

Ko Kyaw Gi, a Burmese migrant worker who has spent time in an immigration prison, said detainees were given old rice and fish marinated in salt to eat. He said that if anyone spilled any rice, the guards would beat and kick them. Injuries among the detainees went largely untreated.

As well as Baling and Alor Star in Kedah state, detention camps exist at Linkay Smone Nyin near Kuala Lumpur and Jodhu prison in Penang.

Migrants "Thrown Away"

Ko Aung Kyaw Set, a Burmese national in Malaysia, said the process by which illegal immigrants were handed over to human traffickers was known as "bwan," or to be "thrown away."

[T]he process by which illegal immigrants were handed over to human traffickers was known as "bwan," or to be "thrown away."

"They are sent to the border. There are those who get back. Some of them are sold to the [fishing] boats. I can tell you for sure that we've been in touch with many of those people. They told us that they didn't have any money for their passage to Burma. They don't have any money to return to Malaysia. While they are caught in between, human-trafficking agents who have bought them sell them to the boats so that they can get back their money."

One Burmese youth in Malaysia said he was dropped with around 150 others at the Thai-Malay border, in the town of Malay Galok in no-man's land.

"There was a small island. There was a river. We were put on a big boat, 150 of us. We were neither on the Thai side nor the Malay side. The island was in the middle. All 150 of us were sent there. The immigration [people] sold us to [the traffickers] for Malay 900 [ringgit] per person. We knew this because they told us, 'We bought you guys.'"

Many Burmese fear trouble from the junta [ruling military group] in their own country, and yet even those with United Nations [UN] refugee status have been found languishing in Malaysia's immigration cells.

"If I were to go back, I think they would still arrest me, so I don't dare go back," a second Burmese youth said. "I have to be on the run. I have no documents. So I still have to be on the run."

The UN High Commissioner for Refugees (UNHCR) cites the presence of more than 30,000 Burmese refugees in Malaysia. In 2006, it said 9,186 persons had active asylum cases pending in Malaysia, of whom 74 percent were Burmese.

Nepal's Struggle with Human Trafficking to India Complicated by the Crime's Fluid Nature

Barbara Gunnell

In the following viewpoint, Barbara Gunnell discusses the trafficking of young Nepalese children. According to the author, they are kidnapped, taken across the border into India, sold into brothels and forced to perform sexual acts. She also discusses the UN Protocol to Prevent, Suppress and Punish Trafficking in Persons, Especially Women and Children, which determines the difference between those being trafficked and those who chose to work in brothels and sweatshops. Gunnell ends with a discussion of how Britain not only ignores the human trafficking in other countries, but also refuses to acknowledge it in their own region as well.

As you read, consider the following questions:

1. According to the International Labour Organisation, approximately how many women and children are trafficked from Nepal every year?

2. According to the viewpoint, what are some main contributions to trafficking?

Barbara Gunnell, "Nothing to Sell But Their Bodies: Everyone Wants to Stop People-Trafficking, but in Impoverished Nepal the Earnings of Exiled Workers, Including Prostitutes, Are the Biggest Single Source of Foreign Exchange," *New Statesman*, vol. 133, March 1, 2004, pp. 32(2). Copyright © 2004 New Statesman, Ltd. Reproduced by permission.

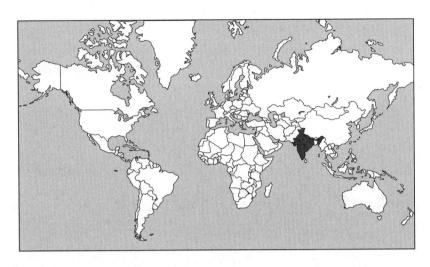

3. As cited in the article, human trafficking makes up the third largest illegal trade. How much profit does it make? What are the other two trades?

"Do you have people-trafficking in Britain?" Ambika Acharya asked. We were in Melamchi village in Sindhupalchowk, a district of eastern Nepal considered particularly vulnerable to trafficking of women and girls for prostitution. Neither of us knew it until the following day but, as she was posing the question, the tragedy of the Chinese cockle-pickers was unfolding in Morecambe.

I answered Acharya's question with a story, published in the *New Statesman* last August [2003], about Chinese labourers working on farms in Norfolk. They were bound to their gangmasters by the debts they had incurred for their illegal passage to England. If they failed to repay the debts in full, reprisals would be taken against their families back in China.

Acharya and the other members of Mank, Melamchi's anti-trafficking group, would have identified with almost every element of the Chinese migrant workers' tale, from the slave-labour conditions to the bondage of debt and the threat to families. The group campaigns in a region with a history of forced prostitution, one where, even a few decades ago, ruling families exercised droit du seigneur [right of a feudal lord to have sexual relations with a vassal's bride on her wedding night] over local girls.

Today, instead, girls as young as ten are kidnapped and taken across the border to be sold to brothels in India. Often their families are complicit. Money may be paid to the family. The brothel will pay the trafficker. The girl will have to earn—with interest—the money the brothel paid for her before she receives anything herself. Sometimes girls who manage to escape report that even after several years the debt remained undischarged.

A common story is for a girl or young woman to be drugged and abducted to the brothels of Kathmandu, or over the Indian border to those of Delhi and Mumbai. Survivors speak of waking from a stupor to find themselves sold into prostitution.

Rita Tamang (a pseudonym she chose herself) tells a typical tale. Nine years ago, she was abducted and imprisoned for some months in a brothel in Mumbai.

"My family is Nepalese, but we went to live in Himachal Pradesh in India when I was five," Tamang tells me in a halting voice. "We ran out of money and moved to Nainital, where my father got work. There, one of his friends tried to convince me to go with him to work somewhere else. I was 17 and said no; I didn't want to leave my parents. Then this person gave me some sweets. I woke up in a brothel but I didn't know that's what it was. I asked the woman in charge what work I had to do: 'Is it washing clothes?' I asked.

"They told me I had to do this sex work, and threatened me with a knife. I wouldn't, so they moved me to another brothel and this time I did. I was there six months and then the Indian government raided us. I was taken by the police to a place called Chempur, which was like a jail. We were there, 150 of us in one room, for seven months, without beds, and no contact with outside. The Indians said they had asked the Nepal government to take us back but it wouldn't. Finally, some charities heard about us and we were split into seven different houses. Those in my house started the organisation Shakti Samuha [now a campaigning group for survivors, working with Oxfam] to help others like us."

Tamang, now free and married (unusually: there is great prejudice against women who have been trafficked), has never found her family. Wasn't she angry with her relatives for failing to protect her from the family "friend"? No, she was convinced that her father knew nothing of what happened.

Other women tell of being deceived by "manpower agencies" that promise lucrative domestic or factory jobs in the Gulf or Hong Kong. Yet others, though it can never be admitted, may find the prospect of working in India's squalid brothels more appealing than an impoverished future in Nepal's failed economy, where more than half the population lives below the poverty line and almost half is out of work for at least part of the year. Nepal spends three times as much each year trying to extinguish the eight-year Maoist insurgency as it spends on education, with the result that only 42 percent of women and 62 percent of men have any reading and writing skills.

The UN Protocol to Prevent, Suppress and Punish Trafficking in Persons, Especially Women and Children (2000) distinguishes between those abducted—for example to work in Indian brothels, or children sold to embroidery sweatshops, circus owners and camel racers—and the self-chosen hardships of illegal immigrants. UNICEF [United Nations Children's Fund] puts it thus: "The smuggling of migrants, while often undertaken in dangerous or degrading conditions, involves migrants who have consented to the smuggling. Trafficking victims, on the other hand, have either never consented or, if they initially consented, that consent has been rendered meaningless by the coercive, deceptive or abusive actions of the traffickers."

But the stories of those who are deceived into prostitution are barely distinguishable from stories of "consenting migrants" who are deceived into paying their passage to a country and a job, but find instead that they are bonded labour.

There are other reasons to be wary of watertight definitions. In Nepal, women's right to migrate in search of a better life has been severely curtailed by the conflation of trafficking and prostitution: the best-funded anti-trafficking charity in Nepal appears to hold that a woman (like a child) cannot consent to prostitution. Thus, any woman crossing the border may be expected to prove that she isn't being trafficked. I spoke to women applying for passports at the Sindhupal-chowk district offices in Chautara. As well as requiring the permission of a parent or guardian, women, unlike men, are interviewed about their intentions and counseled about the dangers they might face. Well-meaning it may be, but the implication is that a woman with a passport must be in search of a brothel.

The conflation of prostitution with trafficking also infects major programmes in Nepal. The United States labour department funds the International Labour Organisation's anti-trafficking programme and will not allow the ILO to use the term "sex work," so Anders Lisborg, an expert on trafficking, chooses his words carefully. The framework of "search and rescue" and the belief that every cross-border bus contains kidnapped women and children destined for Indian brothels is hampering their work, he explains. "Women have a right to the same labour mobility as men. Trafficking is not often about taking someone by force from their village. The main contribution to trafficking is dysfunctional families; alcohol is also a huge problem. Our emphasis has to shift now from interception to prevention and protection."

The ILO is also wary of statistics on trafficking. It suggests that approximately 12,000 women and children are trafficked every year from Nepal but accepts that the figure could be

Initiative to Combat Trafficking in Persons: India

The International Labor Organization's International Program on the Elimination of Child Labor is implementing a project focused on preventing hazardous child labor among migrant children.... Also under the President's Initiative, the United Nations Development Fund for Women (UNIFEM) set up 37 cross-border vigilance groups along the Indo-Nepal border to monitor and prevent trafficking; one transit shelter home was also started at the border. To address sex-tourism in Goa, the Goa project for combating sex tourism focused on prevention training and raising awareness in the tourism industry, including hotels, airlines, and travel and tour operators.

United States Department of State, "Fact Sheet: The President's $50 Million Initiative to Combat Trafficking in Persons: Initiative Highlights," Office of Monitor and Combat Trafficking in Persons, October 15, 2008. www.state.gov.

higher. As India is the main destination, and shares a 1,747km open border with Nepal, it would be unrealistic to look for a precise figure.

Yet however one defines trafficking, the desperate and the naive all have to survive in the same shark-infested waters. Human trafficking attracts annual profits of between roughly $5bn and $7bn and is the third-biggest illegal trade after drug smuggling and gun-running. So it is hardly surprising that, like them, it operates with near-impunity. From Morecambe to Melamchi, the big guns behind the lucrative racket never get caught. Occasionally the middlemen do.

Around the world, remittances from migrant workers— both men and women, and certainly including earnings from prostitution—are the mainstay of economies that have been pauperised and abandoned by the rich world. Nepal's central bank reports receipts of $1bn a year from expatriate earnings, though official estimates necessarily do not include informal ways of repatriating money. Some Nepalese economists claim that the repatriation of earnings from non-resident Nepalis now contributes more foreign exchange to the economy than development aid, which itself contributes more than any local industry, including tourism.

We prefer not to look too closely at the despair that drives people to be insulted and exploited in foreign lands, nor at the dehumanising poverty that pushes women and children into the dangers of prostitution.

Instead, in Britain, we obsess about asylum-seekers and would-be immigrants. We rarely think about the migrant workers already here, their rights, our obligations. They occupy the time and space that we, the legitimate, don't use (the small hours, the backstreets, the hotel basements), but now and then an event such as Morecambe forces us to acknowledge the world we are shaping. We in Europe might like to believe we are having a civilised debate about how many lucky migrants will be allowed to catch crumbs from the rich man's table this year. Meanwhile, Morecambe has shown that we are home to some of the worst abuses from trafficking in human beings. The CIA estimates that in the US there are between 45,000 and 50,000 enslaved women and children, taken there under false pretences and forced to work as prostitutes or servants.

The answer to Acharya's question is: "Yes, we do have trafficking." But unlike poverty-stricken Nepal, we prefer not to do anything about it.

United States Encounters Modern-Day Slavery in Cases of Mistreated Domestic Workers

Lena H. Sun

In the following viewpoint, Washington Post *staff writer Lena H. Sun explores cases of human trafficking and domestic servitude among foreign maids and nannies, many working near the nation's capitol for diplomats or officials of international organizations. Many of the victims suffer physical, sexual, and mental abuse, writes Sun. She investigates how the increase in abused and enslaved domestic employees are prompting workers' rights groups to confront captors and rescue victims.*

As you read, consider the following questions:

1. Why are cities like Washington and New York major destinations for exploited domestic workers?
2. What obstacles do law enforcement officials face when dealing with employers of exploited workers who are diplomats?
3. Why are domestic servitude cases so difficult to prosecute?

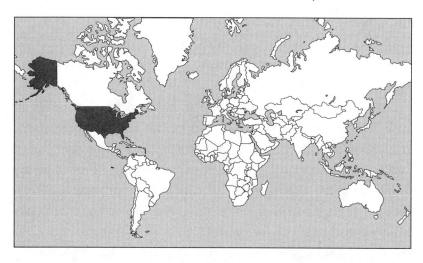

Alexandra Santacruz pressed up to the kitchen window on a recent spring night and peered anxiously down the street. She had done everything she could to get ready, tying her belongings neatly into four plastic bags and hiding them in the trash bin outside the Falls Church townhouse.

Just past 8 p.m., two hours after Santacruz began her vigil, a maroon van eased to a stop in front. Its passengers stepped out to begin their work: They were there to rescue her. The 24-year-old was desperate to leave her job as a live-in nanny, but her employers had threatened to call police if she did.

Two lawyers from CASA of Maryland, a workers' rights group, knocked on the door and confronted her stunned employer. They had become practiced at this exchange, now a common part of their jobs, and they were prepared for the accusations and denials that followed.

In minutes, Santacruz bounded out of the house, an enormous stuffed dog in her arms. "*Estoy feliz!*" she shouted. "I'm so happy."

For nearly two years, she had worked 80-hour weeks cooking, cleaning and baby-sitting for an Ecuadoran official of the Organization of American States. For that, her attorneys said, she was paid little more than $2 an hour. She had worked for the same family in Ecuador, but since arriving, she said, her employer had taken her passport, she had no money and she was afraid that if she left, she would lose her visa and police would come for her.

Stories like hers are increasing among the thousands of women who are recruited every year from impoverished countries as live-in domestic help, according to law enforcement officials and advocacy groups. Now, a growing number of organizations are reaching out to mistreated domestic workers, helping them leave their employers and providing emergency housing and legal advice.

In cases like Santacruz's, the workers suffer years of exploitation. In others, they are victims of trafficking, forced to become modern-day slaves.

A 14-year-old Cameroonian girl was enslaved for three years in Silver Spring by a couple from her country. The two never paid her, and the husband sexually abused her. A Bangladeshi maid for a Bahraini diplomat in New York who was never paid or allowed to leave the apartment was ultimately rescued by police, according to her lawsuit. An Indian maid for a diplomat in Potomac said she was mentally and physically abused and was paid $100 for 4,500 hours of work over 11 months.

An Indian maid for a diplomat in Potomac said she was mentally and physically abused and was paid $100 for 4,500 hours of work over 11 months.

Washington and New York are major destinations for such workers, given their large immigrant populations and because they are home to international organizations, whose foreign officials can bring in domestic servants on special visas. In many cases, the workers are hidden from public view, essentially locked behind closed doors.

"People can't conceive of the fact that modern-day slavery exists here in our own backyards, in the shadow of the nation's Capitol," said Joy Zarembka, executive director of Break the Chain Campaign, an area nonprofit group that focuses solely on domestic workers.

A 2004 CIA report estimates that 14,500 to 17,500 people are recruited or transported into the United States each year through fraud or coercion for sexual exploitation or forced labor. But pinpointing the number is impossible because no federal or state agency tracks the cases.

CASA of Maryland and Break the Chain estimate that they receive a total of 45 to 50 new domestic worker cases in the Washington area each year.

Those who work for diplomats or officials of international organizations face the added threat of losing their visas if they leave their jobs.

Those who work for diplomats or officials of international organizations face the added threat of losing their visas if they leave their jobs.

"It's a really draconian choice," said Carol Pier, the author of a 2001 Human Rights Watch report on domestic workers. "Living in an exploitative situation or leaving your employer to seek justice and losing your legal immigration status."

Worries of Retaliation

For CASA, which has rescued more than 100 domestic workers in the past six years, Santacruz's call set a plan in motion. CASA staffer Silvia Navas talked through the details of her situation in secretive phone calls. They met at McDonald's a few weeks before the rescue and chose a date and a time.

Minutes after Santacruz loaded her bags into the van that night, the CASA crew headed to a nearby townhouse for a second rescue. Germania Velasco, 34, climbed inside the van and embraced Santacruz, whom she knew because their employers both work at the OAS.

"*Estoy siendo rescatada!*" she said breathlessly into her cell phone, assuring a friend that she was fine because she was being rescued.

Inside the house, Velasco's employer, Veronica Peña, and her husband, were shouting at Navas and CASA lawyer Jayesh Rathod. Navas said Peña argued that "everybody's doing this," referring to the low wages paid to domestic help. Navas said she replied, "That's why we're here."

Peña, a second secretary at Ecuador's mission to OAS, said she did not have authorization from her government to comment.

Santacruz and Velasco came to the United States on visas that allowed them to follow their employers. Like many others, they signed contracts that were then ignored by their employers, according to their attorney, Victor Glasberg. Santacruz said she wasn't given time to read the contract and was not given a copy. Velasco's contract promised to pay her $6 an hour, roughly three times what she ended up earning, according to Glasberg.

He is seeking back wages for them—he estimates that Santacruz is owed about $20,000 for 20 months of work and that Velasco is owed $28,000 for nearly two years of work. Under federal wage law, the women could recover twice that amount if their employers knowingly refused to pay the proper wages.

Santacruz's employer, Efrain Baus, first secretary at the same mission to the OAS, refused to comment. His attorney, Samuel G. McTyre, in a recent letter to Glasberg, said Baus and his wife would be "very likely" to settle the dispute if it could remain private. He noted that the couple was surprised by Santacruz's claim and that "she knew the terms and conditions of her employment . . . and agreed to them without any complaint for nearly two years." He specifically denied that they have her passport.

Because the stakes are so high, advocates say, domestic workers are often pressured not to seek redress. The letter from Baus' attorney, for example, mentions that Santacruz's claim "may or may not" affect her relatives' jobs with Baus's family and friends in Ecuador.

Wearing Her Despair

Joy Zarembka, 32, brings a personal passion to her work. She is the daughter of a domestic worker from Kenya. And a few years ago, she learned of a live-in maid in her parents' Gaithersburg neighborhood who had not been paid in five years of work for a Cameroonian couple, according to court documents.

Zarembka had seen the teenager often and assumed that she was the oldest child. "In hindsight, now I can remember the sadness in her eyes," she said. Zarembka's father had contacted CASA, which alerted law enforcement.

Zarembka's outrage prompted her in 2000 to work for a coalition of labor, religious and human rights groups that later became Break the Chain Campaign. The group has since assisted more than 100 domestic workers.

"It takes so little for us as Americans to pay a proper wage, especially when you juxtapose that against the paychecks of the abusers," she said.

Until recently, Break the Chain and CASA were the only groups in the Washington area helping domestic employees. But the growth of the problem has spurred the creation of new groups and new initiatives. With private funding, for example, the nonprofit Project Hope International is planning to purchase two houses to shelter trafficking victims.

Also, a recent emphasis on fighting trafficking, including a 2000 federal law, has freed up federal funding—more than $90 million last fiscal year. With the funds, Break the Chain and other groups, such as Ayuda in Washington and Boat People SOS in Falls Church, have begun training police officers, social workers, nurses, interpreters and others to recognize signs that a worker could be exploited or trapped.

In her training seminars, Zarembka teaches them to ask key questions:

"Are you allowed to leave?"

"Have you been physically and/or sexually abused?"

"Have you been threatened?"

"Do you have a passport?"

"Have you been paid for your work?"

A Vanished Employer

It was a good Samaritan who brought Kurinah Muka to Zarembka and Break the Chain.

Muka had been a live-in maid at an Alexandria high-rise, her days at once tedious and cruel. She was kicked by the woman who employed her, forced to work 19-hour days and allowed to eat only the food that others rejected, she said. For nearly two months of work, she said, she was never paid. Muka described her ordeal in a written statement to immigration officials, who later investigated and said witnesses corroborated her account.

Muka . . . was kicked by the woman who employed her, forced to work 19-hour days and allowed to eat only the food that others rejected . . . For nearly two months of work, she said, she was never paid.

She came from a poor farming village in Indonesia. Her husband's monthly income as a truck driver was about $75. She earned 70 cents a day working on a rice farm.

When a recruiter from an employment agency showed up in September 1999 looking for maids for foreigners, Muka signed up, leaving behind her two young children.

Exploited Household Workers in the United States

Domestics and housekeepers belonged to another group of trafficking victims that for years existed outside the view of law enforcement and society. The jobs "maid" and "nanny" might conjure up benign images and associations. But the TVPA [Trafficking Victims Protection Act] helped increase law enforcement's sensitivity to the possibility that household workers were being trafficked and exploited. It didn't take long for investigators to uncover some egregious cases.

In Arlington, Massachusetts, the neighbors of the well-to-do Saudi couple living on Mystic Street noticed that the household always seemed to have lots of domestic help. . . .

Al Jader [Hana, homeowner] was partial to South Asian maids and by many accounts had used a number of them at her home in Saudi Arabia. . . . One who made the trip was Veronica Pedroza, a Philippines national, who arrived in the United States legally with a temporary visa. . . .

Pedroza and the other women were expected to work and be on call twenty-four hours a day. . . . As soon as the women arrived at the Al-Jader home, Hana confiscated their passports and visas and locked them in a metal cabinet in her bedroom. This was the first level of control she exercised over the women: telling them that if they left the house without their papers, the police would find them and put them in jail.

Anthony M. DeStefano, "Sweat, Toil, and Tears,"
The War on Human Trafficking: U.S. Policy Assessed.
New Brunswick, NJ: Rutgers University Press, 2007.

For three months, she said, she and about 300 other women were held in a camp, with guards at the door to prevent them from leaving. They slept in rooms of 20 women, were taught Arabic vocabulary for cooking and cleaning and told to obey employers. She said she was forced to sign a contract promising her $800 a month, although she was told her real earnings would be $200 to $300.

When she arrived at Dulles International Airport in 2000, she was met by her employer, a diplomat at the United Arab Emirates Embassy in Washington. He told Muka she would be working for a woman who called herself Princess Halla, who later told Muka that the diplomat was the father of her 5-year-old boy and 8-month-old daughter, Muka said.

"My life was misery working for Halla," wrote Muka, who worked from 5 a.m. to 1 a.m. every day.

Halla forbade Muka from bathing because "she did not want my germs in the shower," Muka wrote. Halla often slapped her and kicked her while wearing boots and shoes.

Once, Halla noticed a scratch on the baby's nose. "She pulled a knife out of the drawer and demonstrated pulling the knife across her throat as if to slice it," Muka wrote. "While she was doing this, she looked at me and said that if a scratch occurred again, she would kill me."

Halla confiscated her passport and told her "bad people" would hurt her if she ever left, according to Muka's statement. Muka said she imagined government officials tracking her down.

"I cried every night," said Muka, her face wet with tears as she recounted her story in self-taught English. "I'm praying five times a day."

The breaking point came when Halla "pull my hair, and that's when she scratch my arms and dig with her fingernails," drawing blood, Muka said.

A few days later, Muka fled to a nearby apartment building, where she sat in the lobby until a sympathetic tenant took her in. His daughter downloaded an Indonesian dictionary from the Internet so they could communicate. Break the Chain helped her obtain special immigration status as a victim of trafficking. . . .

Department of Homeland Security immigration officials were able to track the diplomat, but he had returned to the United Arab Emirates, according to an investigator who said he was not authorized to be quoted by name. They could not locate Halla, who used several aliases, the investigator said. Abdulla Alsaboosi, a spokesman for the United Arab Emirates in Washington, said that the diplomat retired and that the embassy was unable to locate him. *The [Washington] Post* was also unable to locate Halla or the diplomat.

Muka eventually found a one-bedroom apartment to share with three other Indonesian women and a job as a nanny for an American family. Under the terms of her visa, she is not allowed to leave the United States for another two years, so she calls her children every Saturday night.

Who Pays for Immunity?

Even when law enforcement officials learn of mistreatment, they can face major obstacles if the employer is a diplomat because many have full immunity, meaning they usually cannot be arrested, prosecuted or sued. Advocacy groups estimate that one third of their domestic servitude cases involve diplomats with immunity.

That was true in the case of a 44-year-old Indian woman who worked for nearly a year as a live-in maid for a senior Asian diplomat in Washington. During her stay at the diplomat's home in Potomac, the woman said, she was abused mentally and sometimes physically by the diplomat's wife, whom she addressed as Madam.

The woman, who refused to be named because she feared retribution, said she worked 16 to 18 hours a day, seven days a week. She said the diplomat sent one payment of $100 to her home in India, the equivalent of 18 cents an hour.

"This Madam, she gave me so much trouble," the maid said in a recent interview. "I didn't do any wrong but all the time she is screaming at me, screaming very bad words, so much bad words."

The maid sought refuge at St. Raphael Catholic Church in Potomac, and the church's outreach coordinator kept the woman's story in a journal. One entry described how the wife pulled her hair and "punched her on the forehead . . . also screaming and cursing."

The maid eventually fled the diplomat's home after she fell ill, but the diplomat kept her passport and belongings, according to Break the Chain. The group said that the woman had grounds to sue for back wages but that the diplomat was protected by immunity. After months of negotiations with the State Department and the embassy, the group obtained her passport and belongings.

With the help of a friend, the maid negotiated with the embassy to reach a monetary settlement last year, but the parties agreed to keep the amount secret, according to the advocacy group.

Chaumtoli Huq, a New York lawyer who won a settlement for the Bangladeshi maid to the Bahraini U.N. diplomat, argues that diplomatic immunity should not take precedence over the constitutional prohibition against slavery and indentured servitude.

"Why should the worker, the lowest of the low, have to bear the burden of immunity?" she said.

Trying Not to Think About It

Domestic servitude cases are difficult to prosecute, law enforcement officials say, because the victims are scared to go to police and the crimes take place behind closed doors. But in Maryland, the U.S. attorney's office in Greenbelt has prosecuted six domestic worker cases in the past four years, all in Montgomery County.

One couple, Louisa Satia and her husband, Kevin Nanji, were each sentenced by a federal judge in Greenbelt to nine years in prison for enslaving a 14-year-old Cameroonian girl in Silver Spring. The couple smuggled the girl into the United States in January 1997, according to court documents and interviews. They promised to send her to school in exchange for domestic work. Instead, she was forced to cook, care for the children and clean. For three years, she was never paid and never sent to school.

Nanji sexually abused her, according to sentencing documents. She wore sweatpants and jeans to bed to make it more difficult for him to take her clothes off. "I would wait for him to go to bed until I could go to sleep," said the worker, now 21, who spoke on condition of anonymity because she did not want friends to know of the assaults.

She wanted to run away, but she had no money or passport. Satia warned her repeatedly that the police would send her away because she had no "papers," according to court documents.

Nearly three years after she arrived in the United States, on the day before Thanksgiving, she fled, shoeless and coatless. She said she begged a woman in the neighborhood for shoes. "She gave me a pair of black flip-flops," she recalled.

She ran to a nearby Kmart and hid in the ladies' room before calling an acquaintance of Nanji's, who found her temporary housing. CASA came to her aid after learning about her from another Cameroonian domestic worker.

Authorities were able to prosecute because immigration investigators found witnesses and travel and bank records supporting their case, Assistant U.S. Attorney Mythili Raman said.

"I try not to think about" what happened, the young woman said. She now is a part-time clerk at an Office Depot. She has received none of the $105,306 in back wages the judge ordered the couple to pay. She is thinking about becoming a geriatric nurse. But first, she wants to earn her high school equivalency degree, a substitute for the education she was promised but never received.

Correction to this article: In some editions of the May 3 [2004] *[The Washington] Post,* certain references in the article about the mistreatment of foreign domestic workers incorrectly implied that two Ecuadorian officials are employed by the Organization of American States. The officials, whose maids are seeking back wages, work for Ecuador's mission to the OAS.

Staff researcher Bobbye Pratt contributed to this report.

Canadian Traffickers Exploit Foreign Workers

Tamara Cherry

While human trafficking in Canada is typically associated with sex slavery, a growing number of foreign workers are being exploited. Toronto Sun *reporter Tamara Cherry explores how such workers are forced into despicable labor conditions. Many victims fall into a situation of debt bondage, deceived by traffickers who promised to find them work. Exploited victims are afraid to speak out for fear of being deported, writes Cherry, their families having made many sacrifices to send them to Canada. This article was among a four-part series investigating how Canada needs to fight trafficking and help victims.*

As you read, consider the following questions:

1. How many case files for temporary foreign workers did Edmonton lawyer Yessy Byl open by the time of her six-month report in 2007?

2. According to Anette Sikka who has worked to combat human trafficking, how would a mandatory orientation help to prevent the types of trafficking occurring in western Canada?

3. While human trafficking victims south of Ontario have been all ages, the large majority fall into what age range?

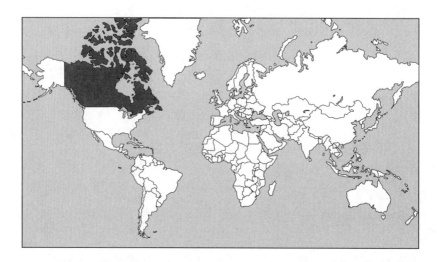

The stereotype is a young woman forced to work in a brothel, strip club or massage parlour.

Reality cuts across all walks of life.

Nannies. Construction workers. Seasonal farmers.

"Nobody knows the language of human trafficking," says Sherilyn Trompetter, assistant executive director of Changing Together, an Edmonton-based NGO [non-governmental organization] that leads the Alberta Coalition Against Human Trafficking.

Many exploited foreign workers are treated simply as employees in poor working conditions, not as human trafficking victims, Trompetter says, pointing to the case of 30 Polish welders who arrived in Alberta in 2005 and 2006 under false pretences and were paid less than half their expected wages.

Many exploited foreign workers are treated simply as employees in poor working conditions, not as human trafficking victims. . . .

"Human trafficking in general in Canada needs to be redefined and it needs to be stated that we've already seen these patterns; these patterns have always existed," she says. "We're just not calling it what it is."

In a four-part series running across the country this week [September 28–October 4, 2008], Sun Media looks at Canada's hidden trade in people; at the failure of this country to live up to its international obligations on human trafficking, to prosecute human traffickers and meaningfully help victims.

Who Are the Victims?

Human trafficking is defined under Canadian law as "the recruitment, transportation or harbouring of persons for the purpose of exploitation," the RCMP [Royal Canadian Mounted Police] writes on its Web site.

Trafficking can be a family member offering up a child to work in Canada as a domestic servant.

It can be a live-in caregiver who is brought into the country and told she will be paid with a roof over her head, not understanding she is also entitled to a wage.

And sometimes, the exploitation is based on false promises, unfulfilled visas and what seem to be a lack of options: A group of trades people who arrive in Canada only to be shuffled to another employer and paid a fraction of what was agreed upon.

"It's often degrees of exploitation," Canadian Council for Refugees executive director Janet Dench says in Montreal. "The more vulnerable people are, the more easy it is to exploit them."

The Alberta Federation of Labour [AFL] moved to address the living and working conditions of temporary foreign workers in 2006 when, for the first time ever, Alberta had more of these workers in the booming province than permanent immigrants.

At the time, there were nearly 22,400 temporary foreign workers in Alberta—doubled from 2003 and tripled from 1997.

The following year, AFL launched the Temporary Foreign Worker Advocate with Edmonton lawyer Yessy Byl at the helm.

By the time of her six-month report, Byl had heard from more than 1,400 people and opened case files for 123 temporary foreign workers "in need of assistance."

"An analysis of the 123 files handled by the Advocate reveals a troubling picture of how Alberta is treating this group of workers," the report said.

"Quite frankly, we are exploiting their vulnerability and taking advantage of their precarious position." The problems can start in a victim's home country, where employment agencies have been known to charge anywhere from $1,000 to $15,000 to process Canadian job applications, says Anette Sikka, who spent several years trying to combat human trafficking in Kosovo before returning to Canada where she is researching human trafficking at the University of Ottawa.

In some cases, agencies are charging workers for skills and language training in their home country and then charging a "settlement" fee upon arrival in Canada—calling it such gets them around provincial provisions that make it illegal to charge for finding employment, Sikka says.

Debt to Pay

Like many trafficking victims who are smuggled into this country, these victims are, too, told they have a debt to pay off. We found you a job, now you owe us some money.

And there is nobody telling them otherwise.

"There's nobody to check up on them," Sikka says.

With no official agreement obligating the federal government to tell the provinces who, when and how many people are arriving as temporary foreign workers or live-in caregivers, employment standards branches across the country, no matter how good their intentions, don't have the necessary information to check up on workers, Sikka says.

"There's no mandatory orientation done," she says. "It's absolutely, 100% necessary. I think it's the primary thing we can do to stop the types of trafficking that are going on in Western Canada particularly." Debt bondage aside, workers can fall into a "vicious cycle" of exploitation simply by not being informed of their rights upon arrival, Sikka says.

Something as simple as informing workers about the procedure of changing employers would be helpful for foreign workers who are granted visas to work at one place, but upon arrival in Canada, are shuffled over to different employers.

By the time they figure out they are working illegally, experts say, these workers may be hesitant to speak out about an exploitive situation for fear of deportation.

"They can change employers if they want, but they're just not told," Sikka says. "Nobody informs them they have to go through that procedure."

"Working Illegally"

"Families who are sending people over, they'll do just about anything: Mortgage homes, take out loans, really just put all their eggs in one basket. So when the person gets here and if the job isn't what they had expected or they're not making the money they had expected or, in some cases, there's actually no job, they've been charged all this money and they end up working illegally," Sikka says. "And then they're stuck in this vicious cycle where they may not be working in accordance to their visa, but they're in such high debt bondage, there's just nothing they can do."

At the International Bureau for Children's Rights in Montreal, program manager Catherine Gauvreau recounts a story that began to unravel a few years ago about a trafficked teenaged girl.

New Enforcement Powers
Under Bill C-49

Bill C-49 (CC Section 279.01–279.04) received royal assent on November 25, 2005. It provides new tools for the RCMP [Royal Canadian Mounted Police] to combat TIP [Trafficking in Persons] within Canada and gives provincial and municipal law enforcement the ability to enforce the new Criminal Code sections. . . .

The criminal law reforms contained in Bill C-49 complement the existing IRPA [Immigration and Refugee Protection Act] trafficking offence and existing trafficking-related Criminal Code provisions. An important element of Bill C-49 is that it does not require the crossing of borders. These new offences will better enable law enforcement to address not only international but also domestic human trafficking cases. Exploitation is the key element of the offence. Canadian law enforcement now has a significantly enhanced ability to ensure that the offence—whether under IRPA or the CC [Criminal Code]—is the one that best responds to the facts of a specific trafficking investigation.

RCMP-GRC (Royal Canadian Mounted Police,
Gendarmeric Royal du Canada), "Frequently Asked Questions
on Human Trafficking," 2006. www.rcmp-src.sc.ca.

Having been separated from her parents during a 1990s conflict in her home country and subsequently separated from her siblings, the girl arrived in Canada with a woman posing as her aunt.

"The child is obviously in a desperate situation in this case. She (the 'aunt') brings the child here, the child goes through the process, is accepted under false identity."

The victim ended up in a home where she "basically does domestic servitude, she takes care of the family, of the children," all the while under psychological control and physical abuse from the family, Gauvreau says.

"She goes into the school system. No one believes her because this is not something that supposedly happens in Canada."

That child, who is now an adult, became a successful refugee claimant after a friend's mother finally found credence in her allegations.

"It's important to recognize that some of the situations are domestic ones, where you have women and men, children even, who are kind of house servants and they're kept in the house and not able to get out," Dench says with this message for the government: "Try to make sure that people have as many opportunities as possible to assert their rights."

Loly Rico, co-director of the FCJ [Sisters, Faithful Companions of Jesus] Refugee Centre in Toronto and president of Ontario Council of Agencies Serving Immigrants, has seen cases of Canadians returning to their home countries to recruit people for work and bring them back to Canada. But instead of paying them money, they pay the workers with food and shelter.

"But they don't let you go out," Rico says.

Of the three trafficked women who have walked into Rico's office this year, two were forced into the sex trade; one was in forced domestic, abusive labour, she says.

"In most of the cases, they have been brought by relatives or friends," she says, adding most victims she has seen over the years come from the Caribbean and Latin America.

Sikka points out domestic and agricultural workers are often excluded from Employment Standards legislation.

Education Needed

"A lot of people want to be involved in trafficking. It's a big, sexy, glamorous, organized crime issue. Whether that's really the case is another story. And I don't think it is," Sikka says. "People don't always want to hear that. It's just not newsworthy, I guess. Because it's been happening for so long and people have ignored it for so long, now that we call it trafficking, they're still ignoring it."

"There's no one that wishes to be in bondage. There's no one that wishes to be confined. And there's no one that wishes to be used."

"It just becomes everybody's responsibility to, in a sense, look out for your neighbour," says Robin Pike, executive director of the B.C. Office to Combat Trafficking in Persons. "If people are suspicious that the live-in caregiver next door has had her passport taken and has never been paid, it really is the eyes of the public."

"The one thing that I think that we should do faster than immediately is the education component," Manitoba MP [Member of Parliament] Joy Smith says. "We should make sure that on airplanes people are warned about human trafficking. We should make sure that there's a 1-800 number if somebody's in trouble, with the resources behind it to make sure that person can be rescued."

"There's no one that wishes to be in bondage. There's no one that wishes to be confined. And there's no one that wishes to be used," she says, adding more resources need to be poured into educating police about identifying victims.

South of Ontario, where a state-wide task force funded by the U.S. government is set up to combat human trafficking, Amy Fleischauer says of the dozens of victims she has come across over the last year and a half, she can't paint just one picture of their situations.

There have been sex workers, restaurant workers, farm workers, domestic workers, says the trafficking victim services coordinator for the International Institute of Buffalo.

"They've been all ages. We've served some minors, but the large majority of our clients have been older, in their 30s and 40s," she says. "There really has been no trend or no one face of trafficking or one characteristic."

Most don't identify themselves as trafficking victims and are referred to Fleischauer by other organizations.

By the time they end up on her doorstep, they want to learn English; they want to know when they can work next; they want employment skills.

"We try to meet those needs and establish some trust and explain their rights and even what their rights are in this country if they're undocumented," she says.

"Those have been some really tough conversations—that even if you are not in this country legally, you can't be beaten."

United Kingdom Wrestles with Trafficking and Sexual Exploitation

Chris Bond

In the following viewpoint, journalist Chris Bond who reports for the Yorkshire Post *explores how human trafficking is becoming an increasing problem in the United Kingdom (UK). Thousands of women and children have been sexually exploited, and many unsuspecting victims are lured to the UK with promises of decent employment. Bond investigates how an anti-trafficking establishment created in late 2006, the UK Human Trafficking Centre (UKHTC), has been tasked to fight the battle against trafficking and rescue victims.*

As you read, consider the following questions:

1. What did Grahame Maxwell, North Yorkshire Police's Chief Constable, help establish in 2006 to fight human trafficking in the UK?

2. According to some estimates, as noted in the article, roughly how many women and children are victims of trafficking in the UK?

3. Why is it easier to lure victims to the UK than to other countries?

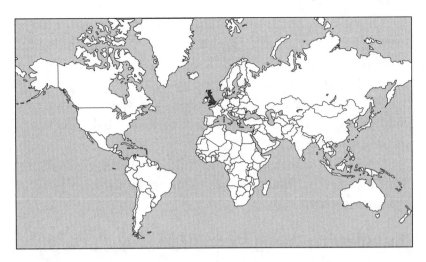

Human trafficking is the fastest growing form of international crime, generating more than £3bn [billion, British pounds] every year in criminal proceeds. It's estimated that as many 800,000 men, women and children are bought and sold worldwide each year.

This abhorrent trade is often seen as something that doesn't affect us, but speaking at a national conference on human trafficking in Leeds yesterday [November 14, 2007], Grahame Maxwell said: "Trafficking is not hidden away down dark alleys, it is taking place on our doorstep."

Only last week [November 4–10, 2007] an Albanian and a Lithuanian were among four people arrested in Leeds on suspicion of human trafficking within the UK [United Kingdom] and controlling prostitution.

The arrests highlight the ongoing battle to smash sex trafficking rings operating in this country.

It's a battle being led by the Sheffield-based UK Human Trafficking Centre (UKHTC), which since opening last October [2006] has coordinated all police anti-trafficking operations that have so far rescued 100 women and children.

Mr. Maxwell helped create the centre and is the UK's most senior officer responsible for tackling this barbaric trade.

Taking time out from yesterday's conference at the Royal Armouries, Mr. Maxwell, who became North Yorkshire Police's Chief Constable in May, said despite several high-profile successes, the problem was not going away.

"Some estimates have said there are 4,000 women and children who are victims of trafficking in the UK in terms of sexual exploitation.

"More and more people we find are being rescued not from massage parlours, but are living in suburbia in terraced houses and flats."

Unsuspecting Young Victims Fall Prey

Some people might find it difficult to understand how someone falls into this trap but Mr. Maxwell admits it can be all too easy.

"One of the first victims we helped in the UK was a 15-year-old Lithuanian girl who found herself in Sheffield where she managed to escape her trafficker and turned up at a police station."

Her case shows how unsuspecting young victims are lured from their homes into a nightmare world of brutality and rape.

"She was phoned up by someone and asked if she would like to sell ice cream for the summer in London and was told she would earn about £300."

The traffickers signed a consent form and her parents, believing it was a good opportunity, approved the trip.

"She was flown to Gatwick and sold in a coffee shop from one trafficker to another for £3,000, her passport was taken off her and sold for £4,000.

"Later the same night, she was taken to a flat and brutalised and raped, and from that moment on she was forced to act as a prostitute."

The girl was sold six times in six different cities in the UK before finally escaping and helping the police catch her traf-

Gangmasters Exploit Migrant Workers in the United Kingdom

Five millionaire gangsters have been identified as key figures in the illegal cockling industry that led to the deaths last week [February 5, 2004] of 19 migrant workers in the dangerous waters of Morecambe Bay in Lancashire.

The gangsters, all British and based on Merseyside, are said to make tens of thousands of pounds a week profit by hiring hundreds of illegal Chinese immigrants on slave wages and making them work in unsafe conditions. . . .

Earning just £1 [British pound] for nine hours of backbreaking labour, the workers would collect sufficient cockles to earn some of the gangmasters more than £20,000 a day. One of these bosses is said to pay neither tax nor national insurance yet lives in a multi-million pound house and drives an expensive sports car.

Anuskha Asthana and Tony Thompson,
"Evil Gangmasters Who Rule the Cockle Slave Trade by Fear,"
The Observer, *February 8, 2004. www.guardian.co.uk.*

fickers who are now serving lengthy sentences. However, once someone is caught up in a cycle of exploitation, it can be hard to break free.

"Quite often they have little or no command of English and clearly they feel threatened by the traffickers. It's the same pull factors whether it's sexual exploitation, forced labour or domestic service—you're made an offer you think you can't turn down."

An Attractive Location

Those responsible are nearly always involved in organized crime.

"Some are UK pimps, while others have international rings like Triad gangs and Vietnamese gangs and there was an Albanian crime gang we took out."

Those responsible are nearly always involved in organized crime.

One of the problems is that the UK is seen as an attractive proposition.

"It's a lot easier to con someone to come to the UK than it is to, say, Estonia, because the perception is the streets here are paved with gold."

The situation is complicated by the growing migrant workforce coming to work here legitimately.

"It makes it more difficult for people in local neighbourhoods to try and identify someone who's not there on a voluntary basis. We have a lot of migrant workers who choose to come to Yorkshire, who get paid the going rate and are quite happy.

"But somewhere underneath there might be one percent being exploited and it's for us to try and identify those people."

Despite these concerns, Mr. Maxwell believes human trafficking is being seen as a serious, international problem. Law enforcement representatives from the United States, Dubai, and Romania were among more than 400 people at yesterday's conference, which he believes bodes well for the future.

"If we'd had this conference two years ago, we would be lucky to have a handful of people and that's the difference I think we've made in terms of raising awareness and it's something we must continue to do."

Periodical Bibliography

The following articles have been selected to supplement the diverse views presented in this chapter.

Arthur Bice — "Government Fights Slave Labor in Brazil," CNN.com, January 9, 2009. www.cnn.com.

B. Bulgamaa — "Mongolia Must Battle Increase in Human Trafficking," *The UB Post*, January 22, 2009. http://ubpost.mongolnews.mn.

Shad Saleem Faruqi — "Blind to Evils in Its Own Backyard," *New Straits Times* (Malaysia), June 16, 2007.

Anne Gallagher — "A Question of Bondage," *The Age* (Melbourne, Australia), May 15, 2008.

Indo-Asian News Service — "Indian American 'Slavery' Couple Sued by Maids," *Hindustan Times*, July 23, 2008. www.hindustantimes.com.

Joseph Rowntree Foundation — "Modern Slavery in the United Kingdom," February 2007. www.jrf.org.uk.

Ethan B. Kapstein — "The New Global Slave Trade," *Foreign Affairs*, November/December 2006. www.foreignaffairs.org.

Barbara Kralis — "Modern Day Slavery Flourishes," RenewAmerica, July 19, 2006. www.renewamerica.us.

Susan Chaityn Lebovits — "Nobody Is Paying Attention," *Boston Globe*, August 20, 2007. www.boston.com.

Kim Seong-kon — "'All the Brothers Were Valiant,'" *The Korea Herald*, July 2, 2008.

Rebecca Wynn — "SA Hotbed of Human Trafficking," *Mail & Guardian Online* (South Africa), June 5, 2007. www.mg.co.za.

CHAPTER 3

The Global Problem
of Sex Slavery

A Brief History of Sex Slavery: An Overview

Rosemary Regello

The following viewpoint, written by Rosemary Regello—editor and publisher of San Francisco's The City Edition, *takes a look at the history of sex slavery, with evidence dating from ancient Greece to the present. The report investigates crimes such as the white slave trade of the nineteenth century, "comfort women" used during World War II, the demand for sex slaves seen with the collapse of the Soviet Bloc, and more recent scandals involving United Nations troops and contractors. The battle against sex slavery continues, as women and girls are being lured by traffickers and falling victim to sex slavery, including debt bondage prostitution.*

As you read, consider the following questions:

1. What is the Mann Act?
2. According to the viewpoint, how did the business model of former World Bank President Robert MacNamara impact the downtown areas of many developing countries?
3. Why did the Trafficking Victims Protection Act (TVPA) create a loophole for traffickers with regard to prosecution?

Herodotus and other ancient historians tell us the Greeks were famous for carting off young women after battles. The human booty was consigned to lives of servitude, either as concubines or domestic servants.

In Rome, at the height of its far-flung empire, one in every three persons is thought to have been a slave. Like the Greeks, most were captured in foreign wars. While most men toiled as laborers, girls and women were more likely to be channeled into entertainment avenues.

In Rome, at the height of its far-flung empire, one in every three persons is thought to have been a slave.

It's interesting to note that prior to 4000 B.C., or what has been dubbed "pre-history", evidence of sexual servitude and slavery are largely absent from the artifacts of human culture. And following the Indo-Aryan invasions into the Near East at around that time, evidence suggests that the temple sexual rites common to the Neolithic Age were converted into a practice far less consensual and now involved the payment of money. Hence, the business of prostitution was born, not of prostitutes, but of pimps.

[T]he business of prostitution was born, not of prostitutes, but of pimps.

Selling Women, a Profitable Business

During the African slave trade, already well underway by the 13th century, women fetched prices much higher than that of men. In the 19th century, the sexual appetite of the southern plantation owner here in the United States also figured into the picture, and this abomination, perhaps more than any other, stirred the conscience of New England abolitionist Harriet Beecher Stowe, whose *Uncle Tom's Cabin* helped ignite the Civil War.

By the turn of the 20th century, a white slave trade had sprung up in Europe and North America, involving thousands of young women who were transported as sex slaves, sometimes to Mexico. The White-Slave Traffic Act of 1910 was adopted to prosecute the criminals. Better known as the Mann Act, the F.B.I. [Federal Bureau of Investigation] has been using it ever since to prosecute anyone who transports a prostitute across state lines (i.e. domestic trafficking).

Across the Atlantic, European feminists of the time raised hell because so many of their own governments had been implicated in sex slavery schemes. International treaties were adopted in 1904, 1910, and 1925 outlawing the trade in women.

Japan's Comfort Women

Returning to the battlefield, in World War II, the Japanese army surpassed the inhumanity of even the ancient Greeks when it enslaved a quarter million women in sex camps to service its soldiers. The women came from Korea, China, Burma, the Phillipines and Indonesia. About half died from injuries, illness and starvation at the hands of their captives.

Unlike the concentration camps in Europe, however, the plight of the *jugun ianfu*, or comfort women, went largely unreported in the media. General [Douglas] MacArthur classified official documents implicating Japan, although some of the material was later recovered and presented in legal proceedings seeking compensation for the surviving victims.

At first denying any government knowledge or complicity in the scheme, Japan eventually issued what many victims thought to be a lame apology. It also established a small, first come-first served "Asian Women's Fund". The Philippines likewise allocated some money to help a number of its own women who had suffered all their lives, many in silent shame. But the vast majority of victims have yet to receive any compensation for being raped hundreds, even thousands of times.

In 1949, another treaty outlawing trafficking in women was adopted by the international community. Remarkably, the United States was among the few countries that refused to ratify it.

The Business of Sex Tourism

In the 1970s the U.S. Military tossed its trousers into the prostitution business when Secretary of Defense Robert Mac-Namara arranged for cities in Thailand and elsewhere to establish brothels for thousands of U.S. servicemen fighting in Vietnam. Of course, the women in these ventures were to be paid and not forcibly enscripted.

After the first Gulf War in 1991, the *New York Times* reported on a navy fleet as it dropped anchor at Pataya, Thailand, which had maintained its sex work operation over the years. Thousands of Thai girls were waiting as the crews disembarked from their ships. (So were some distraught military wives, tipped off in advance about what was happening.)

Sex tourism, as it was dubbed, proved so lucrative for all parties concerned that MacNamara brought the business model with him when he took over as head of the World Bank. According to researchers investigating child prostitution in the 1980s, MacNamara's revamped bank loan requirements had transformed the downtown sectors of many developing countries into red-light districts.

The idea was to generate badly needed foreign exchange by enticing western men to visit places not normally included on the Club Med circuit.

In the nineties, nonprofit organizations mustered their forces to try and address the growing problems of trafficking and child prostitution worldwide.

A group called Equality Now began badgering the New York district attorney to prosecute a sex tourism company called Big Apple Oriental Tours. Although the first case was

Israel's Fight Against Sex Trafficking

Marina—not her real name—was lured to Israel by human traffickers. . . .

[She] came to Israel in 1999 at the age of 33 after answering a newspaper advertisement offering the opportunity to study abroad.

"I was taken to an apartment . . . , and other women there told me I was now in prostitution . . . and then others there raped me.

"I was then taken to a place where they sold me . . ." she said, recalling how she was locked in a windowless basement for a month, drank water from a toilet and was deprived of food. . . .

She managed to escape, but the physical and mental scars remain.

Raffi Berg, "Israel's Fight Against Sex Trafficking,"
BBC News, November 6, 2007. www.news.bbc.co.uk.

dismissed by a judge in 1993, the group persisted, and a second case eventually put the company out of business.

Big Apple had arranged sex tours for men to the Philippines. The Dominican Republic, Thailand, India, and Sri Lanka are other popular destinations. Men routinely swap details about individual prostitutes they've patronized around the world, posting reviews on the Internet.

Increasing Demand

In Western Europe, the market for sex slaves skyrocketed with the collapse of the Soviet Bloc in 1991. This was the first time since the white slave trade of the 19th century that the world had seen so many Caucasian women bought and sold for the purpose of sex.

At this time, brothels also became big business in Israel. Owners were importing so many trafficked women from the Ukraine and elsewhere in Eastern Europe that it prompted stories in the *New York Times* and on NBC's [National Broadcasting Company's] *Dateline*.

In response, the United States and the Netherlands jointly funded a media campaign to warn women in Eastern Europe about scam employment offers and other means of luring women into debt bondage prostitution that were being employed by traffickers.

An international conference in Vienna in 1996 called for tougher sanctions, and in 2000, the Convention against Transnational Organized Crime was adopted. Also known as the Palermo Protocols, about 80 nations signed and ratified the new treaty, including the United States under the Clinton administration.

However, Congress made an end-around the treaty by adopting the Trafficking Victims Protection Act (TVPA) that same year. Rather than protecting victims, as its name implies, TVPA created a giant loophole for traffickers by requiring prosecutors to prove "force, fraud or coercion" with regard to the prostituted women.

The international treaty states that consent of the victim is irrelevant in trafficking.

The Bush administration claims it has secured over 100 convictions under TVPA in the last six years. Yet none of the 45 suspects in the 2005 California brothel raids was tried or convicted under the TVPA law.

Since 2000, prostitution scandals involving U.N. [United Nations] peacekeeping troops and defense contractors have been plentiful. In Liberia, U.N. administrators were implicated in a scam where food aid was used to force girls and women into servicing peacekeeping troops and local businessmen.

In 2002, a Dyncap employee testified to Congress that fellow workers stationed in Bosnia had bought girls to keep in their homes as sex slaves. Although the Bush administration declared a "zero-tolerance" policy regarding such activities, the company went on to receive a no-bid contract the following year to provide police, justice and prison functions in post-conflict Iraq.

Asian Women Are Lured to Australia and Forced into Sexual Servitude

Leonie Lamont

Leonie Lamont reports in The Sydney Morning Herald *on a disturbing trend in Australia: young Asian women, promised decent jobs, are being trafficked into the country and enslaved in debt bondage prostitution. This is an organized operation, Lamont conveys, where young women are forced to work as prostitutes to pay off their debts to brothel owners, who in turn pay the traffickers as well as the agents who recruited the girls for false employment opportunities. While Australia is making strides to combat trafficking, greater support for getting sex slave victims to come forward is needed, as is improved visa protection.*

As you read, consider the following questions:

1. How much money a month were the two Indonesian victims "Eti" and "Yosien" promised they could earn working in an Australian restaurant?
2. According to the Thai student interviewed, what was her typical work schedule every day?
3. Why do many of the women working in Australian brothels hope to get caught by immigration?

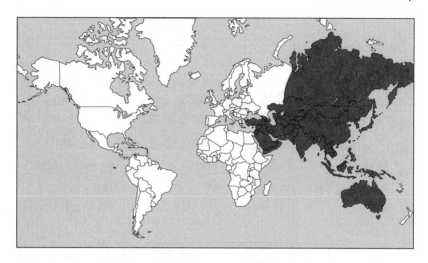

It was an upstairs bedroom: a double bed, massage table and, in the dim red light, a "beautiful" curtain on the rear wall. A middle-aged woman pulled the curtain aside to reveal twin doors. Low in one door a hole had been cut, and beyond was darkness.

The girl with her was ordered through the hole, into a storage area which was packed with cardboard boxes, and another room with mattresses on the floor. Weeks later, police would find the hole in the wall, which, unbeknown to passersby, created a link between the brothel and the building next door.

The goings-on in those two buildings are just one example of something evil under Sydney's nose.

Forget the red-light seaminess of Kings Cross. These brothels, some of them licensed by local councils, exist in Sydney's residential heartland: Annandale, Marrickville, Rozelle, Strathfield, Surry Hills, Homebush, Penrith and Ryde.

Although the extent of sexual servitude in Australia is unknown, more stories are emerging of young Asian women being lured on false promises, only to end up working as sex slaves in a strange land, with little English, no passports and no freedom.

The 20-year-old Thai student thought she was coming to Australia as a waitress, but said that 24 hours after arriving, she was put to work. Three Indonesian girls were luckier. Before being put to work they escaped from an inner-west red-brick unit and, in the middle of a winter's night, ran through the back streets begging motorists to stop.

[M]ore stories are emerging of young Asian women being lured on false promises, only to end up working as sex slaves in a strange land, with little English, no passports and no freedom.

Before escaping they had allegedly been under the tutelage of a woman identified by police as one of seven people charged in Sydney and Melbourne on sexual slavery charges.

Young Women Lured into Debt Bondage

The women say they are either duped or agree to work as prostitutes, but once they arrive in Sydney their passports and airline tickets are confiscated, they are confined and forced to pay "debts"—on average, about $45,000. Some, like the Thai student, believed that $200,000 changed hands.

One Indonesian woman, a prostitute who spent time in another inner-west brothel, was blunt: "This was not what I had expected. I would never have come to Australia if I was to be treated like this. I felt locked up like an animal, had no freedom . . . I felt totally trapped and unable to think of a way to escape."

The girls are a commodity. The brothel owners take about 60 percent of the half-hourly rate of $120–$130; the rest goes towards their debt. The girls keep their tips. "Just put up with it and you will finish your debt within one year," the Thai student recalled being told by another girl.

The trail to Sydney for escapees "Eti" and "Yosien" started in April last year [2003] when they travelled from their small

Indonesian village to a neighbouring village to consult a soothsayer. One wanted guidance about caring for her sick mother; the other advice about a business opportunity.

As fate would have it, the psychic had died, and the girls were sent on a bumpy bus journey to another village. A man identified as Sutikno told them of their good fortune: they could make 10 million rupiah [Indonesian currency] a month ($1509), plus tips, working in a restaurant in Australia.

The girls are a commodity. The brothel owners take about 60 percent of the half-hourly rate of $120–$130; the rest goes towards their debt.

When Eti was taken to the airport in Jakarta, she was met by "the boss"—a Chinese-Indonesian middle-aged man—who allegedly handed her a false passport, visa and boarding card. The immigration officer let her through, but kept the $160 bribe hidden inside the passport. He joined her on the flight.

Yosien had made the journey two weeks earlier. Instead of a restaurateur, she was met by a man who took her passport, allegedly telling her she was going to work in a sex shop and would have to work 400 hours in this arrangement to pay him back. He added that if she was not choosy, she would be able to pay the debt off in three months.

Forced to Work Day and Night

The girls frequently have no idea of the size of the debt, and it bears little relation to the actual outlay of the traffickers. When they arrive the girls work off the debt to the brothel owner, who pays the traffickers and agents who recruit the girls.

Financial records found during an investigation by the Australian Federal Police and their Thai counterparts into the most recent instance of sexual slavery show the owners of

Sexual Servitude for Sale in Australia

Since 2003, when new legislation on sexual servitude was introduced in Australia, the Australian Federal Police have investigated 43 cases of trafficking. . . .

In 2000, in response to growing awareness of the global problem and some well publicised cases in Australia, legislation was updated outlawing slavery and servitude.

However, there was still no specific offence of people-trafficking, which was not in line with new internationally agreed standards set out by the UN [United Nations] trafficking protocol. . . .

Bruce Hill, national manager of border and international network for the Australian Federal Police . . . acknowledges that trafficking for sexual servitude is a difficult area in which to prosecute. "Witnesses can be discredited—they are being treated as prostitutes in the witness box. And it is hard to give a prostitute creditability."

Suzanna Clarke,
"Sexual Servitude for Sale,"
The Courier Mail, *March 18, 2006, p. 53.*

two suburban brothels transferred $48,000 in three months to the Bangkok account of a woman trafficker.

The Thai student was also recruited by a woman, whom she knew as "Aunty Pui". Pui allegedly said she could earn $150 a week at the restaurant, and, while living free on the premises, could repay the airline ticket from her wages.

After their arrival, the girls are groomed and tarted up with trips to Paddy's Markets. The Thai student said she was shown a black see-through dress and new red G-string when she arrived at the Annandale brothel.

"All the windows had bars on them and I couldn't get out ... I sat on the sofa and cried. I thought if I was a virgin I would never do it, I would prefer to kill myself." Her first customer had a shower. "I explained I did not want to have sex with him, he didn't say anything but continued to have sex with me. I cried during the whole time I was in the room with him." She was anally raped by another customer.

After a week she was allegedly sent to another brothel owner. "There were 15 girls who lived at the [inner-west] house—three bedrooms and five girls each room. Jack [the minder] sleeps in another room. Jack drives all the girls to the brothels. Every day I worked 9 to 4am the next day." She would be told how much she had to make every day: "It varies from $400–$1000," she told police.

The student was given $20 for food for the week. Jack's shopping trip netted her canned tuna, six eggs, four packs of noodles, a bottle of milk and some oranges.

Another girl, also duped into thinking she was to work in a restaurant, found the penalty for refusing to work was to go hungry. "If I didn't work I wouldn't get any food ... The last day I had any food was midday two days earlier," she told police.

Supporting Women to Come Forward

The trafficking puzzle is being investigated by Operation Tennessee, an operation run by the federal police and Department of Immigration. Legislation introduced four years ago provides for jail terms of up to 25 years for those involved in sexual servitude.

Kathleen Maltzahn, the director of the Melbourne-based advocacy agency Project Respect, said those involved in the trade of sex slaves sometimes include women who had originally been trafficked. Girls tended to be more trusting of women, which made it easier for them to be duped.

"In the past people really couldn't believe it was happening. People now are more aware and are picking up the signs, from police through to customers," she said.

Maltzahn believed the cases now coming before the courts showed the state and federal government agreement last year to combat trafficking was working. But while the visa protection arrangements had improved, they were still deficient. "We need to look at how we support women to come forward, and while we have a witness support program rather than a victim's support program it's hard to do that," she said.

Escape can be daunting, but not impossible. The Thai student was rescued by police after calling 000 when the brothel's reception was briefly unattended. Another Thai girl, "Vivian", who was allegedly locked up after hours in a brothel at Strathfield, rang a customer, begging him to call the Department of Immigration.

Even working prostitutes see an Immigration raid as the only way out. "Cherry" arrived in April last year [2003] and saw 160 clients before she was picked up the next month as part of Operation Tennessee. All she'd seen of Melbourne was the one-bedroom high rise she was locked in with five other girls, and the daily chauffeured car journey to the brothels. The one night out at karaoke and three shopping trips had all been under escort.

"The girls and I hoped that we'd get caught by Immigration, as it was the only safe way we could see to get home," she said.

Romanian Sex Slaves Are Failed by a Challenged Law Enforcement System

E. Benjamin Skinner

In the following viewpoint, author E. Benjamin Skinner illustrates the brutality of sex slavery in Bucharest, Romania, recounting how he was offered a seemingly disabled woman in exchange for a used car. Skinner learned about slavery in a Quaker Sunday school as a young boy. While working as a writer for Newsweek International, *the author met his first survivor of slavery. He later set out to travel the world in search of other victims, and found humans being sold on four continents. Skinner is a graduate of Wesleyan University. He published his book* A Crime So Monstrous *in 2008.*

As you read, consider the following questions:

1. In Bucharest during the 1990s when orphanages closed, where did many children end up?
2. Roughly how much did the author figure the used car to be worth that he described to Florin in exchange for the female victim?
3. How does the justice system in Romania differ from the American system, according to the author?

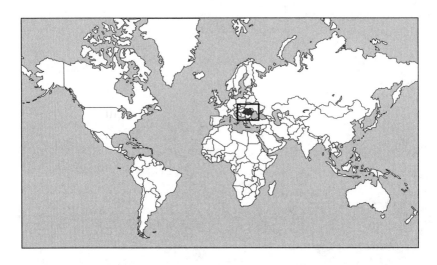

Petrică Răchită and Alexandru arrived. Petrică, thirty, was a hard-nosed, no-bullshit journalist with deep contacts in both the underworld and the police. He was not a talker, but in the month that I would spend traveling with him, I saw up close that he was a natural democrat, the brave embodiment of a new young Romania. Though forced to wave Ceauşcu's banners in parades as a child, he was disgusted with the past. Yet he, along with a small, vibrant segment of his countrymen, radiated hope that they could change their country.

Alexandru, his cousin, was a fresh-faced twenty-one-year-old agriculture student, who spoke excellent English and would be my translator. As Alexandru smoked and wired me for sound, Petrică drained a tumbler of Scotch and explained he wouldn't be able to go into the slave sale with me. This was a surprise, though I knew that Petrică's colleagues had been threatened and attacked for writing about police corruption. Recently, in the area of our investigation, Petrică had tangled with the new Romanian special police, the *mascaţi*. The masked shock troops had an ugly record of unchecked violence, including summary executions. . . .

In front of a black strip club by the J.W. Marriott Hotel, Petrică stopped, explaining that was as far as he could go because the *mascaţi* had blown his cover during a prior investigation. Now his car, as well as his face, might trigger a violent reaction from the brothel owners. Ion, an underworld contact of his, would guide Alexandru and me from here.

A minute later, Ion pulled up, slouched behind the wheel of his late-model Opel, beautifully customized with leather interior and a crackling bass tube.[1] He didn't say a word, but smiled and, as was the custom in Bucharest, parked on the sidewalk. Ion was a *haiduc*, a term loosely translated as "brigand" but there is no direct English equivalent for the big-hearted, Robin Hood-type thief that it connotes. Romania has always maintained an easy attitude toward petty crime. Thanks to the battalions of computer engineers left unemployed after communism, Ion's racket, credit card fraud, was a well-staffed industry.

Petrică turned to me with a final word of advice before he disappeared. "Speak low, but not too low," he said. "Some Gypsies speak English, but even if they don't, they will be suspicious if you whisper. Any problem, call me. I call the police."

We were about to enter an area of Bucharest untouched by Western anti-trafficking efforts. I did not know who I would be negotiating to buy, but I guessed that she was an unregistered aftershock of the recent explosion of internal migrants who made Bucharest Europe's most densely populated city. Some found their fortunes here. Others, invisible, were slaves.

Ion drove to the Gara de Nord rail terminus. During the 1990s, as the orphanages closed, more than a thousand children made their home in cardboard boxes near heating vents in this station. In 1998, Bucharest officials purged the kids, but pedophiles already had staked out the area. Older children, who kept the visitors' money, pimped younger children,

---

1. I have changed Ion's name.

ho received candy and glue. The kids lived in the sewers, and serviced the clients in grotty apartments or at the nearby Hotel Ibis, well known to middle-class Romanian men and budget-conscious sex tourists.

We crossed the street to a public park, where homeless men and women slept on benches. Two filthy, glassy-eyed boys approached to beg. They peeked out above the plastic bags they held to their faces as they huffed Aurolac, a paint thinner that quickly numbed the hunger pangs in their stomach while it slowly destroyed the cells of their brains and livers. One boy had burns on his forehead, perhaps from where the caustic smear had touched his skin.

For two cigarettes, a boy slurred out the place to purchase a girl. We got back in the car and Ion drove around the corner to Șoseaua Orhideelor, in the *quartier* Basarab, one of the most loathed ghettos in Bucharest. In this area, Ceaușescu had forcibly resettled the lowest in society, the Roma, in the mansions of the highest in society, wealthy foreigners, who subsequently went back to their home countries. The government still owned 90 percent of the buildings here, but planned to demolish many to build an overpass.

We got out in front of a ramshackle nineteenth-century town house situated between a shoe store and a tire repair shop. Alexandru was uneasy; this was a new line of work for him.

A Romani woman with a hatchet face jumped up from a folding chair in front of the building. From her hair color, she might have been in her mid-thirties. From her permanently frantic expression, wiry frame, and rotting teeth, she might have been in her mid-eighties.

"Florin!" she shouted.

Around the corner came a Gypsy, short and, like his partner, wild-eyed and aggressive. Florin's nose was smashed, his arms lithe and muscled; but his hands were stocky and short, making his fists perfect spheres. He had a receding hairline, an underbite, stubble. He wore a yellow watch, shorts, and an unbuttoned navy blue shirt. Scattered on his arms and left thigh were dark green jailhouse tattoos. Though his entire torso was emblazoned with a faded multicolored dragon, he was known as a *peşte*, a fish—Romanian street slang for pimp.

There was no phatic communion, no "How are you?" no "*Cu plaçere*," not even a hello.

"I want to buy a girl," I explained through Alexandru.

"How much are you offering?" Florin responded, deadpan.

"That depends on what the girls look like," I said. "Can we come inside?"

Through a banged-up sheet-metal gate, we stepped onto a courtyard of crumbling, exposed brick that reeked of mold. Squealing toddlers played in the muck on the ground. A large woman with a baby on her chest sprawled on a mangled sofa in front of a single-story annex.

"Gagicuţe!" Florin shouted.

From the annex emerged a frightened-looking young Romani girl in hotpants and a tank top.

"The most I can give you her for is one week," said Florin.

"I'm thinking more long-term," I said.

"Two weeks?"

"I want to buy a girl *outright*," I explained. "How much would that be, and what's the cost basis? How much would you be making other wise?"

Florin shook his head.

"Not possible?" I asked.

"Not more than a month. And for a month is a lot of money—a thousand Euros."

"I want to buy her for good," I said.

"No. Just for rent. For a week, okay. One week, two weeks, tops. You won't find a girl to buy anywhere in Bucharest. For her, not more than a month and a half."

"How old is she?"

"Twenty," said Florin, surely overstating her age by at least four years.

"I'm looking for someone a bit younger," I said.

"We also have a blonde" the hatchet-faced woman interjected.

"In a room upstairs. But just for an hour—or two, three, four, or five. But just here, just here in the room. She knows how to do a good job. She is good," said Florin.

"They don't seem very eager to sell her," Alexandru explained quietly. "They say they'll be losing money."

"I want to find out how much money," I said.

The hatchet-faced woman led us into the back of the shoe store, up cement stairs to a landing, where she told us to wait. The toilet green walls cast all in a sickly hue. In keeping with the toilet motif, the place smelled of feces and dead mice. Clear plastic tubes ran sewage along the sides of the stairwell, expelling it onto the concrete courtyard below. Maybe it was just the normal choke of an average, fetid urban cave in Bucharest, but it seemed there was some miasma here, wet and pungent. If, as Cicero said, slavery was death, then this was a charnelhouse.

Then, a scream from above us. A fat woman with orange hair pulled back in a gold loop emerged and talked fast.

"She doesn't want to come," she said. "She's scared, she thinks you're going to beat her or sell her again."

The fat woman went back upstairs. "Make her come out!" she yelled.

We walked to the second floor, where two women shouted into a darkened room. A third woman emerged, clutching the girl.

She had bleached, rust-colored hair. Her head was shrunken, her nose flattened against her face. Mascara ran from pools of tears around deep-set eyes, cast downward at her bare feet with widely spread toes. Her hastily applied makeup could not conceal the evidence of Down syndrome.

Undercover Team Experiences Slave Trade in Bucharest

At night, the rooms above a building in downtown Bucharest resemble a scene straight from the 18th century slave trades, and it's taking place in front of *48 Hours'* hidden cameras.

There, correspondent Peter Van Sant is negotiating to buy a human being—not for an hour, but forever. . . .

Posing as traffickers from America, *48 Hours'* crews went undercover, hoping to rescue a victim of this insidious industry. . . .

"You can buy 10 girls in one night, if you want to. You can say I want a 13-, a 16-, a 17-, and a 21-year-old, and you can buy them all like that," says Iana Matel, who runs a shelter for trafficking victims outside Bucharest. . . .

She says that many of the girls on the street look like prostitutes but are actually slaves, ready for purchase and export to Western Europe or the United States. . . .

48 Hours decides to do business with [in] trafficker, Nadia, who says she has a young, blonde girl for sale.

Nadia brings out the girl, "Nicoleta", to meet with Van Sant. . . .

Nicoleta undresses, "They usually show the girls to see she doesn't have any marks, any skin disease so they can show she's good to be used," says Matel. "It's, like, when you say, sell a cattle in the market."

"To you, it's a human being. To them, it's not," adds Matel. "To them, it's income. It's a way of making money."

CBS News, "Rescued from Sex Slavery,"
48 Hours, *February 23, 2005. www.cbsnews.com.*

Lipstick was smeared beyond the boundaries of her parted mouth. Her flesh rolled out of the tight yellow tank top and shorts. Her captor held her left arm so tightly as to hunch her shoulder. Below her right bicep were no less than ten deep, angry red slashes, raised, some freshly scabbed.

I had been in a dozen seedy brothels on three continents, but I had never seen anyone in such a condition. I remembered that I was wearing a wire, that I had to keep in character. But what would my "character" do when confronted with such a creature? Should I be enjoying myself? I tried to smile. I looked at Alexandru and Ion's faces, which betrayed sheer horror.

"Do you like her?" one of the women asked.

"Can I talk to her?" I asked. "How old is she?"

"Twenty-eight," the woman said on the girl's behalf.

"What type of price are we talking about?"

Her captor asked if she would go with me. The girl mumbled something, which Alexandru couldn't make out exactly, about being hit.

"She said yes," the woman said.

"I think she's really scared," Alexandru said. "She doesn't want to come."

"Okay, why don't we go talk to the guy about price, then," I said, as we turned to leave that place.

Downstairs, Florin was locked in an argument with his partner. I couldn't make out the words, but I heard *caşcaval*—a term that I knew meant "cheddar" or "cash."

"There is nobody that will give you a girl for as much time as I will," he said. "For two months, two thousand Euros."

"What are the rules?" I asked.

"No rules. Whatever you want to do. Two months."

"Two thousand Euros? I don't understand, because you wouldn't be making two thousand off her in two months. That seems high."

"That's not a lot. For one night, I make two hundred Euros off her."

Lying to *gadje*, or outsiders, is a Romani tradition. Later, police deduced that each of Florin's customers, probably locals, paid the *peşte* around 10 Euros. They also surmised that the girl was raped five to twenty times per night. Florin's estimate was therefore feasible, if high-end.

"Tell me a bit more about the girl. I want to know more about the product that I'm buying," I said.

"She's very clean. A very nice girl—you won't have any problems with her. Whatever you say, she will do. Anything you want."

"Two thousand seems like a lot," I said.

"No, for two months that's very inexpensive!" The whiff of a big sale woke him up. "The girl is very nice, she is not doing drugs. She is good at what she is doing."

"How about something else?" I proposed. "A trade. A motorcycle—I can see that being about the value."

"A car, maybe. Not a motorcycle. A good car."

"A Dacia?" I proposed, offering the local make.

Florin's eyes lit up.

"But only if I'm buying the gift for three months," I added. "And the car will come with fifty thousand kilometers." The car I'd described, I figured, might cost 1,500 Euros from the right chop shop.

"Okay," Florin said, revealing a stained grin for the first time.

"I've got to call around," I said. "Could I leave the country with her?"

"What if you leave me with my eyes in the sun?" he asked, employing a Gypsy expression for being stood up. "I don't know if you'd be back with her. I need a deposit. But I can get a Romanian passport for her."

I shook his hand and we returned to the car. . . .

Beginning in the 1990s, human trafficking metastasized faster than any other form of slave-trading in history. As many as 2 million people left their homes and entered bondage every year. Some crossed international borders; many did not. Human beings surpassed guns as the second most lucrative commodity for crime syndicates of all sizes, netting around $10 billion annually.

Thanks to that meteoric growth, American abolitionist efforts dwelled on trafficking. Meanwhile, contemporary slavery as a whole received a sliver of the concern it deserved. Thanks to the Horowitz coalition sex slaves dominated Washington's anti-slavery bandwidth. Meanwhile, fewer than half of all trafficking victims were forced into commercial sex work.

But when Florin agreed to trade a severely handicapped young woman—who had repeatedly tried to kill herself to escape unyielding rape and torture—for a used car, I understood the Bush administration's single-mindedness. It was a wave of nausea, and a wave of clarity. . . .

[W]hen Florin agreed to trade a severely handicapped young woman—who had repeatedly tried to kill herself to escape unyielding rape and torture—for a used car, I understood the Bush administration's single-mindedness.

Worldwide, most sex slaves, like the girls in Florin's Basarab brothel, are below government radar. Sometimes they are illegal aliens, worried about deportation, and kept as a subculture within a subculture. Such was the case with the Nigerian trafficking victims I interviewed in Amsterdam's largely West African Bijlmer district. Sometimes the lost victims have been in the same land for centuries, but form a nation within a nation.

"It is difficult to enforce the law in Romani communities," said Alina Albu, one of Romania's most successful anti-trafficking prosecutors. Like Petrică Răchită, she was young, passionate about her country, and dedicated to justice despite personal risk. But Albu was also frank about the shortcomings of the Romanian legal effort. Although the number of Romani traffickers had exploded in the last five years, there were no Romani police officers specialized to work with their own communities. Romani slave traders were a distinctively brutal and evasive lot, as Albu explained when I told her about Florin. "They have *their* law. The victims don't cooperate. The traffickers are more violent than Romanian traffickers because it's in their culture, their blood."

Although the number of Romani traffickers had exploded in the last five years, there were no Romani police officers specialized to work with their own communities.

Say the police raided Florin's brothel and took the girls to a shelter. He could have them back in a day if he maintained he was the primary caregiver, and the mentally handicapped girl, clearly traumatized, failed to testify. Under the Romanian system, no testimony meant no prosecution, even with the evidence that I had on my wire. "If I don't have a victim to present in front of the judge," Albu said, "I don't have a case."

Convictions Are Difficult

Getting victims to testify was the most daunting obstacle to nailing slave dealers. The problems started on contact, when local police treated prostitutes like low-level criminals, not victims. A woman who was raped and enslaved by a man she initially trusted was then asked to trust a detective she had never met before. Add to the problem that, for decades, the Romanian police were the most odious element of a vile state. Add, too, that the justice system in Romania is one where prosecutors are "objective" investigators and not, as in the American system, advocates seeking to justify the state's interest in the criminal activity of the accused. Add that pimps told victims that if they talked to police, they or their families would be killed. Add that shamed clients, whose role was never punished, rarely testify even as witnesses.

The sum of those circumstances revealed just how remarkable it was that Albu was able to win any convictions at all. She credited American pressure for forcing national leaders to confront the problem: trafficking was made illegal only after the TIP office put Romania in Tier Three. Since then, American trainers—FBI agents and Justice Department attachés—provided guidance. But Albu herself derived her tenacity from a personal calling.

"I have a daughter," she said.

London Has Become Europe's "Sex Slavery Capital"

Emma Thompson

Oscar-winning actress Emma Thompson speaks out against sex slavery in the following viewpoint. Promoting the art installation, The Journey, *and asking for signatures on a petition imploring the government to ratify the European Convention Against Trafficking, Thompson urges Londoners to help bring about change. England is considered the European "capital" for sex slavery, she argues, with the majority of sex workers trafficked into the country. Thompson is the chair of trustees for the Helen Bamber Foundation, an organization helping victims of trafficking and exploitation.*

As you read, consider the following questions:

1. As explained by Thompson, what is the art installation, *The Journey*, helping to demonstrate?

2. Why do traffickers immediately confiscate their victims' passports as they arrive in Britain?

3. According to the author, what portion of England's sex workers come from abroad?

Let's talk about sex. Because here in Britain we've got a serious problem.

The other day I took my seven-year-old daughter into WH Smith [retail store] and realised as we walked down the maga-

Emma Thompson, "Sex Slavery Shames Our Country," *The Mirror*, October 11, 2007. www.mirror.co.uk. Reproduced by permission.

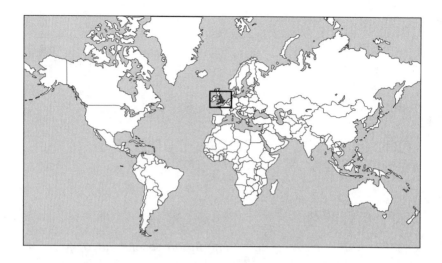

zine aisle that piles of bare naked ladies, boobs and all, were smiling out at her from the covers of lads' mags.

Exactly at her eye level, naturally. What sort of message is that sending out?

Then there are the billboard adverts for cars or perfume or ice cream that further degrade women as sex objects.

I'm not being prudish. It troubles me. Because when it comes to the sort of sex forced upon the 4,000 women currently selling themselves after being carted into Britain, people don't want to know.

It's one of our last taboos.

As chair of the Helen Bamber Foundation—a UK [United Kingdom]-based human rights organisation which is helping to rebuild the lives of victims of sex trafficking—I have been moved to tears by the tales of these unsuspecting women.

Raped, beaten and imprisoned for weeks on end in grotty [British slang for grotesque, miserable] flats across Britain, they find it hard enough to speak when we're actually listening.

Shamed into silence by traffickers, they are scarred both inside and out.

Exhibition Brings Harsh Reality to Light

But last week [October 2007] in London's Trafalgar Square—and next week in Liverpool and Glasgow—the harsh reality is there for all to see.

An exhibition called *The Journey* uses seven crates—the kind used to smuggle women into Britain—to trace how a sex slave ends up servicing around 40 clients a day.

Make no mistake, this isn't just art. It's going on behind closed doors all around us.

The bedroom scene hit me hard. The stench of stale sex engulfs you as you enter through a curtain of "used" condoms. It's gut-wrenching.

A single bed covered with a filthy, graffitied sheet pulsates to the sound of a man groaning.

And when I look in the mirror, where a tally of punters [customers] is drawn up in cheap red lipstick, I think of the countless women who have told me about similar hovels.

One girl I got to know, a 19-year-old from Moldova, was shut away in a room for three weeks. She had been dumped in London after arriving in the UK where she knew nobody.

The loneliness broke her down. It's a standard trafficking trick. Nothing better than a bit of isolation to make a woman comply.

The first thing a trafficker does is confiscate the victim's passport on their arrival in Britain.

From that moment on she is powerless. It's a myth that all of these criminals are men—many are former sex slaves themselves who have lost all sense of self-respect. They have been forced into acts that revolt their every sense.

It sounds like something from a film, but this is a real-life nightmare taking place on streets across Britain every night of the week.

Women Freed in Massive Police Raid

Three women held as sex slaves in Scotland were bought for just £7000 [British pounds]—and forced to have sex with up to 20 men a day.

Human traffickers charged up to £60-a-time for sex with the victims . . .

They were among 17 sex slaves rescued during a series of raids across Scotland in the last few months. . . .

[O]ne senior officer said the slaves were being treated like "used cars". . . .

The recent raids took place as part of Operation Pentameter 2, a UK-wide effort to free women from the clutches of organised crime gangs.

Tom Hamilton,
"Sex Slaves Bought for £7000 Freed in Police Raid,"
The Daily Record, December 27, 2007. www.dailyrecord.co.uk.

Not Prostitutes

A decade ago 85 percent of workers in British brothels were UK citizens, but today the same proportion come from overseas.

England is now thought to be Europe's sex slavery capital, with three quarters of sex workers coming from abroad.

But please don't call these tragic human beings "prostitutes". To hear them described like that offends me deeply, because there is not a bone in their body that wants to be doing what they are doing.

They see thousands of men a year because their "owner" has told them they owe up to £25,000 [British pounds] for being brought to Britain—sex is to be their job.

It's dubbed "the oldest profession in the world", but a woman I met at the Foundation taught me something new. The lesson goes back to my teenage years.

I have always lived in the same part of London. As a schoolgirl I used to walk past a massage parlour round the corner from my house.

It was a seedy place with greened-up windows. I'd giggle with my friends as we went past saying, "It must be a knocking shop!" To us, it was a different universe.

But this new friend I've made just in the last year was enslaved in that very building for months.

I wonder how'd be if we swapped places. She too had a family once. All that was taken from her. And yet she has been brave enough to open her mouth and speak out about the hideous things men have made her do.

When I first got interested in campaigning for these people I used to think, "If I could only find them, I could help."

And here she was, working on my doorstep. It makes me feel very frustrated.

Around 14,000 people came to see *The Journey* at Trafalgar Square earlier this month and many more are expected to see us in Glasgow and Liverpool. So far, we have collected 10,000 signatures to support our petition asking the Government to ratify the European Convention Against Trafficking.

On issues like this, being famous can help get things done. But only so far.

The fact is that I'm a Londoner. And I hate the fact that it is now home to this ruthless secret robbery of women's lives.

The fact is that I'm a Londoner. And I hate the fact that it is now home to this ruthless secret robbery of women's lives.

Less than a mile from *The Journey*, in the red light district of Soho, it's happening.

This year is the 200th anniversary of the abolition of the slave trade. Just look how far we've come.

Something needs to change.

United States' Anti-Prostitution Campaign Usurps Federal Program to Fight Slave Trafficking

Joel Brinkley

Joel Brinkley's following article questions the relationship between prostitution and slavery. He argues that President George W. Bush's administration has pursued an ideological anti-prostitution campaign—wherein every prostitute is considered a slave—and has cut off funding to aid groups that failed to make prostitution a part of their charters. This has resulted in a misdirection of efforts, and real victims of human trafficking are left behind, he contends. Brinkley is a professor of journalism at Stanford University and a former Pulitzer Prize-winning foreign correspondent for the New York Times.

As you read, consider the following questions:

1. According to the Bush administration, roughly how many people are trafficked into slavery each year?
2. In the Melissa Farley study that Brinkley references, what were the greatest needs identified by 75 percent of the prostitutes surveyed?

Joel Brinkley, "An Obsession with Prostitution," *The Sacramento Bee*, January 11, 2008. www.sacbee.com. Copyright © *The Sacramento Bee* 2008. Reproduced by permission of Tribune Media Services.

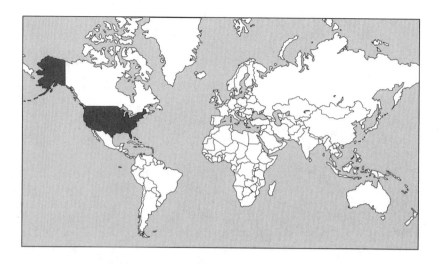

3. Why does Brinkley believe that former Ambassador
   Nancy Elly Raphel was forced out as director of the federal trafficking office?

During the waning days of the [Bill] Clinton administration, the Central Intelligence Agency published a ground-
breaking study that said at least 700,000 men, women and
children around the world are trafficked into slavery each
year. New estimates since then have gradually increased the
count. But if the [George W.] Bush administration is to be believed, the actual number is closer to 7 million.

Slave trafficking victims are usually promised a good job
in a distant country. But once they arrive, they are held against
their will and suborned into sweatshop or agriculture labor,
domestic servitude or forced prostitution. It is that last cat-
egory, sex slaves, that the Bush administration has distorted to
the point of absurdity.

Put simply, the administration has concocted the view that
every prostitute, worldwide, is actually a slave; the very nature
of the work amounts to slavery. That nonsensical position is a
favorite of the Christian right, and a few years ago the admin-

istration enshrined it in law and began cutting off funding to aid groups that refused to make opposition to prostitution an official part of their charters.

[T]he administration has concocted the view that every prostitute, worldwide, is actually a slave.

Prostitution or Slavery?

Two federal judges ruled the law illogical and unconstitutional, but the Justice Department appealed.

The result has been to pervert the federal program to fight slave trafficking in the United States and abroad. Under Bush it is largely a campaign to abolish prostitution.

Ambassador John Miller headed the federal Trafficking in Persons office when the prostitution policy was first enforced in 2003. Before he left office last year [in 2006], I once asked him if he believed every prostitute is, de facto, a slave.

"No," he said, drawing out the word. "If you take the Melissa Farley study, in eight or nine countries including the U.S., 89 percent of prostitutes say they want to leave" the job. "So I guess you can say 11 percent are not slaves." Even then, he added, "50 percent of those are under 18. The law says they are slaves. So that means the vast majority of them are slaves." Farley runs the Prostitution Research and Education organization in San Francisco, and her work serves as the intellectual basis for the federal policy. One study found that 89 percent of prostitutes interviewed in nine countries said they would like "to leave prostitution." Is that a surprise? Did the study find that, to leave, they would have to be freed from the people who enslaved them? No, 75 percent of these women said their biggest needs were job training and a new home.

Those don't sound like the primary concerns of slaves.

Prostitution—Not Always Slavery

A current legislative fight is underway about just what slavery means. Over the objections of a few anti-slavery stalwarts in the Justice Department, the House of Representatives passed a bill in December [2002] that expands the current anti-trafficking legislation to cover most forms of prostitution, coerced or not. If approved in its current form by the Senate and signed by the president, the law will no longer address slavery exclusively and will instead become a federal mandate to fight prostitution on a broad scale.

Prostitution is always degrading, and it is often brutal—but it is not always slavery. Equating the scourge of slavery with run-of-the-mill, non-coerced prostitution is not only misleading, it will weaken the world's efforts to end real forced labor and human trafficking.

E. Benjamin Skinner, *"Slavery's Staying Power,"*
Los Angeles Times, *March 23, 2008. www.latimes.com.*

I asked Farley if she thought Washington was distorting and conflating her work. She believes prostitution is an abhorrent, dehumanizing practice that should be abolished. But to my question, she said: "I don't use the word slavery; it conjures up an image of a naked person on the dock. I am not going to diss the trafficking office, but that word gets in the way of what I am doing." This would be an interesting academic argument but for the hundreds of thousands of people worldwide who are, in fact, enslaved, including farmworkers forced at gunpoint to harvest crops for no pay, women imprisoned as domestic slaves and then sexually abused, sweatshop workers locked in the factory at night and beaten if they try to escape.

An Illogical Argument

The Bush policy seems to care little for these victims and instead pursues its ideological anti-prostitution campaign. Ask any of them to justify their view, and they will say, as Miller told me: "You've got to face the fact that you can't have sex slavery without prostitution." That's a nonsensical syllogism [reasoning based on a general premise to deduce a narrow conclusion]. You can't have child molestation without children. So should we abolish kids? You can't have bank robberies without banks or auto theft without cars. For that matter, you can't have murders without people. The whole argument is absurd.

The Bush policy seems to care little for these victims and instead pursues its ideological anti-prostitution campaign.

I haven't asked the current director of the federal trafficking office, Mark Lagon, how he feels about this issue. But it's not possible to hold the job without endorsing the prostitution campaign.

The first person appointed to head that office seven years ago, Ambassador Nancy Elly Raphel, was forced out because she disagreed.

"It was so ideological," she told me. "Prostitution, that's what was driving the whole program. They kept saying, 'If you didn't have prostitution, you wouldn't have trafficking.' I was happy to leave." Lagon is not making that mistake. Speaking to an international audience last fall, he offered his view: "The demand for commercial sexual exploitation is the driver that we have to address in dealing with sex trafficking."

"If there were not demand for the purchase of women and girls," he added, "there would be no sex trafficking."

Periodical Bibliography

The following articles have been selected to supplement the diverse views presented in this chapter.

Suzanne Fournier "U.S. Slams Canada's Record on Sex Trafficking," Canwest News Service, Canada.com, June 4, 2008. www.canada.com.

Alan Johnson "Horror of Teen Sex Slavery Not Foreign Woe; It's Here," *The Columbus Dispatch*, January 25, 2009. www.dispatch.com.

Helen Kinsella "Will Ireland Become a Soft Touch for Traffickers?" *The Irish Times*, November 22, 2008. www.irishtimes.com.

Karen Kissane "Madam or Slave Owner?" *The Age* (Melbourne, Australia), May 17, 2008.

Donald G. McNeil Jr. "Girls Sold as Sex Slaves Are AIDS Risk, Study Says," *New York Times*, July 31, 2007. www.nytimes.com.

William Sparrow "Philippines Exporting Labor and Sex," *Asia Times Online*, March 15, 2008. www.atimes.com.

Tiraspol Times Staff "Official Involvement in Moldova's Human Trafficking and Sex Slave Trade," *Tiraspol Times & Weekly Review*, June 14, 2007. www.tiraspoltimes.com.

Alan Travis "Sex Trafficking Victims Rescued by Police May Face Deportation," Guardian News, October 4, 2007. www.guardian.co.uk.

John Whittet "Sex Slavery: Living the American Nightmare," MSNBC.com, December 22, 2008. www.msnbc.msn.com.

The Harsh Reality of Child Slavery

Child Labor Exploitation: An Overview

C. Nana Derby

In the following viewpoint, C. Nana Derby provides a framework for understanding contemporary child slavery. Derby argues that millions of children throughout the world are slaves—many are born into a life of bondage, while others are kidnapped or sold by their parents. Millions more are laborers, robbed of a normal childhood and confined to a life of poverty and hazardous working conditions. Derby draws distinctions between traditional and contemporary slavery, and clarifies the definitions of child labor and child slavery. Derby is an assistant professor in the department of sociology, social work, and criminal justice at Virginia State University.

As you read, consider the following questions:

1. In terms of their relative worth, how do contemporary slaves differ than slaves of the past?

2. What are the basic features common to slavery in general, as described by the author?

3. What are two rites of passage commonly associated with children being engaged in certain economic activities?

C. Nana Derby, "Child Labor Exploitation: The Slavery of Our Time," Paper presented at the annual meeting of the American Sociological Association, San Francisco, CA, August 14, 2004. Reproduced by permission of the author.

Child slavery lives with us today. It is different from other types of slavery; ... the differences present obstacles to understanding the extent and causes of child slavery today. This problem arises because the framework and definitions of slavery currently used in sociology and anthropology, though interesting and sufficient to cover older (historical) situations, are unable to describe adequately the contemporary conditions of child slavery. There is also a vague, if any, distinction between child labor and child slavery. One is usually left to wonder also if child labor is synonymous with child slavery, or with child labor exploitation. The deficiency in definition, in particular, makes it difficult to discuss child slavery in any meaningful way. It also makes it difficult to coordinate the practical work being done to combat child labor exploitation in general. . . .

Distinctions Between Contemporary and Traditional Slavery

Generally, the slave is a person who has lost, or never had, her or his freewill, and is usually subjected to violent threats. The source of this lack of freewill is one of the differences between contemporary and traditional slavery. Slavery emerged from war captivity. War captives were spared their lives in order that they would provide free labor for their captors. Over the years, and until its abolition, slavery became ascriptive. Children born to slaves usually were denied their rights as humans. They were the natural possessions of their parents' masters. They did not have their freewill, and suffered the same violent and dehumanizing treatments that their ancestors had suffered. The new slave, nevertheless, does not have to be born to slave parents. These are otherwise free women who, through their pursuit of greener pastures on foreign lands, become enslaved by human traffickers; kidnapped children or those who are either given away, sold or pawned by unsuspecting parents or other relatives; and children who are forced into military conscription. Contemporary slavery thus stems from economic destitution, poor governance, lack of access to information and the general vulnerability of women and children, rather than through one's birth.

The ascriptive nature of traditional slavery makes it permanent, unlike the new slaves. This permanency is well documented. What is missing in the literature is the understanding of the reality that slaves could be partially owned, as is characteristic of contemporary slavery. . . . The contemporary slave is exploited and disposed of when they cannot generate any incomes for their exploiters. In India, for instance, creditors usually ask for replacement when bonded children become indisposed and less able to work long hours. Additionally, contemporary slaveholders are not obliged to maintain their victims. In fact the victims lose a significant proportion of their incomes to their perpetrators as payment for over bloated living expenses.

The contemporary slave is exploited and disposed of when they cannot generate any incomes for their exploiters.

Another factor distinguishing the two types of slavery is their relative worth. Old slaves were very expensive. The slave of the 19th century cost between US50,000 and US100,000 [dollars] per person in today's currency, while the contemporary slave may be obtained without cost. Most of them are victims of kidnapping and trafficking who usually have to part with huge sums of money in order to free themselves. . . .

The last distinction between contemporary slavery and the traditional is the role that race and ethnicity played in the enslavement of some people. In the past, it was the norm for slaves to be obtained from 'outside' groups, which were racially or ethnically defined. Apart from the few instances of traditional slavery in places like Mauritania, economic vulnerability is the single most important factor leading to the enslavement of others in societies.

. . . It is observed that certain basic features are common to slavery in general. These include the loss of freewill, subjection to violent threats and abuse, the absence of a remuneration that is commensurate with work done, working long hours and the inability for the victims to volunteer their participation or not in the assigned tasks. . . . Children's work is enslavement if they are not knowledgeable of the tasks and or mature enough to understand the intricacies of their employment. This position, coupled with those slavery attributes mentioned earlier make it possible for us to understand why most of what is categorized as child labor is in actual fact slavery.

[M]ost of what is categorized as child labor is in actual fact slavery.

Contemporary slaves may not go through the same processes of war captivity as the old slavery. Nevertheless, they lose their free identity through processes that may not be so different from the old slaves. Contemporary slaves, although originally recruited probably as domestic helps or farm hands who would otherwise be as free as other members of the households they may be working for, get to be socialized to adopt slavery identities. . . .

Child Labor vs. Child Slavery: Clarifying the Continuum

I define child slavery as "the coercive engagement of children's labor under conditions that conflict with the victim's cultural practices, compel them to work long hours without proportionate remunerations, deprive them of their rights to formal education and their free will to volunteer participation in the said occupation." The concept of "child labor" is often used

Child Labour and Education

Child labour not only represents a severe obstacle to school attendance, it also interferes with the educational performance of children who combine school and work. . . . In a number of countries they represent the majority of working children.

Country	Children involved exclusively in economic activities	Children studying only	Children combining economic activity with school	Children neither involved in economic activities nor attending school
Bangladesh	9.1	78.4	7.7	4.8
Cambodia	8.6	36.5	43.7	11.3
Colombia	2.8	83.0	9.4	4.8
Ecuador	3.0	81.7	11.3	4.0
EI Salvador	2.8	80.9	6.0	10.3
Ghana	10.4	63.7	18.1	7.9
Guatemala	7.7	62.4	12.3	17.5
Honduras	4.8	79.2	6.6	9.4
Kenya	3.0	70.7	3.7	22.6
Malawi	4.9	58.7	22.7	13.7
Mali	37.6	20.4	33	9.0
Mongolia	3.5	82.9	3.8	9.8
Nicaragua	4.8	75.9	7.3	12.0
Panama	1.5	91.7	2.5	4.3
Philippines	2.0	83.8	11.3	2.9
Senegal	11.5	51.6	7.1	29.8
Uganda	3.7	47.8	40.4	8.0
Zambia	9.6	65.8	3.6	21.0
Zimbabwe	1.7	76.8	12.6	8.8

TAKEN FROM: Federico Blanco Allais and Frank Hagemann, "Child Labour and Education: Evidence from SIMPOC Surveys," International Programme on the Elimination of Child Labour (IPEL)—Geneva, June 2008.

interchangeably with "child slavery". However, slavery is distinctly different from labor exploitation, although the former could be subsumed under the latter. Their usage therefore presents nothing short of ambiguity to our audience and readers.

This lack of clarity between child labor and child slavery has come as a result of four interrelated factors. I identify the synonymous use of child labor and child slavery as the first factor militating against any concrete conceptualization of the use of children's labor in exploitative ways that could be defined as enslavement. It is logical that the concepts of 'child labor exploitation' and 'child labor abuse' are used correspondently, given common sense notions of "labor exploitation" and "labor abuse". Exploited children might work long hours, are probably denied the chance to participate in formal education and might never be remunerated for the services provided. Nevertheless, child slavery cannot be used interchangeably with the concepts of child abuse and child labor exploitation. Slavery goes beyond mere labor exploitation. . . . Children's immaturity, their lack of understanding and knowledge of the circumstances under which they work are the best explanatory factors of their enslavement.

The second source of confusion is the dual nature of children's work, as is perceived within the international community. Children's work may be negative or positive. However, the use of the concept of 'child labor' ordinarily implies unacceptable use of children's energies in industry, agriculture, domestic services and prostitution, just to mention a few. It refers to the exploitative use of children's labor, which occurs in different forms. They may be forced to work long hours, paid less or be forced to carry out strenuous tasks for which their fragile bodies cannot support. Positive children's work, on the other hand, is identified in terms of their overall contributions to the child's socialization, their subsequent integration into societies and the expected or potential contributions that such socializations would make towards the individual's welfare, that of her or his family and the entire society's. . . . The contribution of children's work to the welfare of their families cannot be overemphasized especially in the third world. Poverty in these regions often compels parents to allow their children to work.

In addition, some cultures perceive children's engagement in certain economic activities as a part of their socialization and rites of passage. Such rites vary among different cultures. The common ones are naming ceremonies and puberty rites. Through children's work, societies instill in their young, work expectations and conformity to the general social order. The children are provided with skills, which in turn enable them to contribute to their families' incomes. . . .

The third reason for the confusion relates to the illusion that slavery no longer exists. This illusion has blinded us to the use of children's labor under slavery conditions. It is consistent for 'child slavery' to be considered a component of 'child labor exploitation'. However, there is a great dissimilarity between 'child slavery' and 'child labor'. In their general use of the concept of 'child labor' to represent children's labor exploitation and slavery, the United Nations (UN) and its subsidiaries including the ILO [International Labour Organization] have almost failed to highlight any distinction between child slavery and child labor. In fact some of what the ILO defines as child labor is virtual slavery. . . .

Commercial sexual exploitation, bonded labor, armed conflict and child domestic labor are mostly slavery. Historically, a number of characteristics are identified with any labor relationships that can be seen as slavery. These include the loss of free will, the subjection of the victims to control through violent threats and long hours of work without commensurate remuneration if paid at all. Rationally, when children's labor is exploited without the loss of free will and control through long hours of work and violent threats, the victims could only be said to have suffered repressive labor exploitation. The worst scenario is for them to be underpaid. Nevertheless, when underage children are bonded and bullied to work, at times in hazardous occupations, while being put through physical and verbal abuses, they cannot be categorized as merely exploited wage laborers, but slaves.

Ghanaian Fishing Industry Relies on Child Slaves for Dangerous Work

Tara Boyle

In the following viewpoint, Tara Boyle, staff writer for Washington File, *discusses the growing problem of child trafficking in Africa. According to the article, child trafficking in Ghana has been most common. Boyle focuses the article on Togbega Hadjor, a chief within Ghana, and his efforts to end the exploitation of children. The article also explains that the prevalence of child trafficking in Ghana has been driven mainly by economic need.*

As you read, consider the following questions:

1. According to the article, how many children have been rescued from forced labor in Ghana's Lake Volta?
2. As stated by the author, how many people have been abducted in Sudan since 1980?
3. In Togbega Hadjor's opinion, what besides economic need is a cause of child trafficking?

For the scores of boys who work in the fishing industry on Ghana's Lake Volta, life is more than simply grueling and monotonous—it is slavery, with no schools, no medical care, and no hope.

Tara Boyle, "Child Trafficking a Major Problem in Africa, Report Finds: Ghanaian Chief Describes Efforts to Combat Child Labor," *The Washington File*, June 15, 2004, pp. 1(2). U.S. Department of State, Washington, DC.

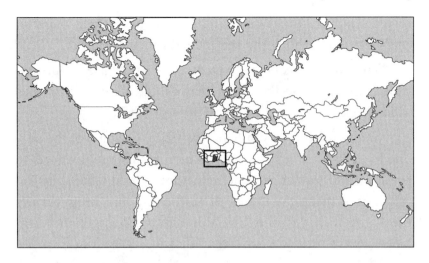

The boys, some as young as six years old, have been sold by their families to spend their days rowing boats across the lake and pulling nets laden with fish from the water.

More than a year ago, Togbega Hadjor, paramount chief of Ghana's Bakpa Traditional Area, where child trafficking has been common, committed himself to ending this exploitation of children when the International Organization for Migration (IOM) asked for his help in combating child slavery in the Lake Volta region.

Hadjor was among several heroes in the fight against human trafficking who were honored in Washington June 14 [2004] when the U.S. Department of State released its annual Trafficking in Persons Report. The report evaluated efforts by 140 countries around the world to combat human trafficking, and ranked countries in tiers that correspond to their efforts to end the practice.

When the IOM approached him, Hadjor put together a list of 13 villages in his region where child trafficking was taking place, and held community meetings to discuss ways to reintegrate boys who had been working in the fishing industry. Over the past year, 228 children have been rescued from forced labor on Lake Volta, and Hadjor has helped many of them enroll in school and reunite with their families.

"The problem is being overcome. When I have people approach me, I advise them that they should remove their children [from slavery], and they've been doing it," he said.

Among nations in sub-Saharan Africa, Ghana was the only one to be listed as a "Tier One" nation for its strong efforts to prevent child trafficking. The report found that Ghana has excelled at protecting victims of trafficking and reintegrating them into their communities, although it still urged the Ghanaian government to pass anti-trafficking legislation.

Three nations in sub-Saharan Africa—Equatorial Guinea, Sierra Leone, and Sudan—received a "Tier Three" or least favorable ranking in the report for failing to make reasonable attempts to end the exploitation of minors. In Equatorial Guinea, the report found, the government has not used the resources from its petroleum industry to do anything to alleviate the situation. In Sierra Leone, it said, the government recognizes that trafficking is a problem, but has not made substantial efforts to prevent it.

The report was particularly critical of Sudan, noting, "Government officials deny the existence of trafficking in Sudan." It is estimated that 17,500 people have been abducted in Sudan since 1980.

Nations ranked as Tier Three face the possibility of losing U.S. aid if they do not make an effort to combat human trafficking. Globally, 10 countries were included on the Tier Three list.

The report indicated that child trafficking is a particularly challenging problem in Africa because of the practice of "fostering" or "placement" of children. Under this traditional system, children are sent to live with relatives or other trusted individuals, and are given schooling or learn a trade. Yet "in all

Many Lake Volta Child Slaves Find Freedom

In 2001, Monika Parikh, a researcher for Free the Slaves, traveled to Lake Volta in Ghana. Her aim was to explore rumors of children being enslaved in the fishing villages there. . . . These children, some as young as three, work long hours mending, setting, and pulling nets; cleaning and smoking fish; and rowing the fishing boats. The greatest danger comes when they must dive deeply into the lake to retrieve snagged nets. The fishermen tie weights to the children to help them descend more quickly. If not drowned outright, the children suffer from shock when forced down into water that is too cold for diving. . . .

For all the horror these children suffered, a happy ending to this story is unfolding. After Parikh completed her research, she circulated it to a number of local and international agencies. . . . With a large grant from the U.S. government, the IOM [International Organization for Migration] set many of the children free and reunited them with their families. To prevent recurrences, the IOM helped the fishermen move into other types of work if they promised to stop enslaving children. Once the children had been returned home, their families were also helped to find ways to increase their incomes, thus relieving some of the pressure that drove them to "sell" their children in the first place. To date, more than a thousand children have been freed, and the nature of the fishing industry on Lake Volta has been transformed.

Kevin Bales, Understanding Slavery Today,
Berkeley and Los Angeles, CA:
University of California Press, 2005, pp. 10–12.

too many cases, the child is trafficked into a situation of forced domestic servitude, street vending, or sexual exploitation," the authors wrote.

In Ghana's Bakpa Traditional Area, where Chief Hadjor has helped reunite children with their families, trafficking has been driven by economic need. Communities downstream from Lake Volta that once supported themselves through farming and fishing have been left destitute by the construction of two dams on the Volta River, and many families that sent their children to work on the lake did so because they could no longer support them.

Hadjor sees another underlying cause of child trafficking: polygamy. Men who marry several wives and have large families often find themselves unable to support their children, he said.

"I tell [villagers] that if you want a wife, take only one," he said.

(The *Washington File* is a product of the Bureau of International Information Programs, U.S. Department of State. Web site: http://usinfo.state.gov)

Côte d'Ivoire's Child Slaves Are Hurt—Not Helped—by Chocolate Boycotts

Jeremy Kahn

Jeremy Kahn investigates how the civil war in Côte d'Ivoire has divided the country and is hindering efforts to improve child labor practices. The civil war is perhaps the greatest obstacle to ending child labor in the chocolate business, Kahn argues, and while many well-intentioned consumers believe that a chocolate boycott will help end child slavery on cocoa plantations, it will only hurt the economy, and in turn, the children they are trying to protect. Kahn is a writer in Washington, D.C., former managing editor of The New Republic *magazine, and former writer at* Fortune *magazine.*

As you read, consider the following questions:

1. What is the Harkin-Engel protocol?
2. How has the Security Council intervened with punishments in the civil war?
3. What percentage of the population now lives in poverty since the civil war began?

L ate last week [February 7–10, 2007], Teun van de Keuken, a Dutch journalist, walked into an Amsterdam court and did something strange: He asked a judge to jail him for eating

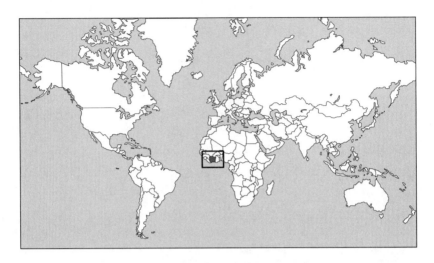

chocolate. The stunt was part of a long-running effort by van de Keuken to draw attention to abusive child-labor practices in the harvesting of cocoa, the main ingredient in chocolate. By eating chocolate, van de Keuken argued, he was abetting child slavery. "If I am found guilty of this crime, any chocolate consumer can be prosecuted after that," van de Keuken told Reuters. "I hope that people would stop buying chocolate and thus hurt the sales of big corporations and make them do something about the problem."

So far, the sins of van de Keuken's sweet tooth haven't landed him in the slammer. But his hijinks are well-timed: Today [February 14, 2007] is Valentine's Day, a key holiday for chocolate sales, and van de Keuken at least made headlines. Every year since 2001, when stories first surfaced about child slavery on cocoa plantations in Côte d'Ivoire—where about 40 percent of the world's cocoa is currently produced—activists have used Valentine's Day as an occasion to push for a boycott on chocolate. Their concern makes sense: A 2001 U.N. [United Nations] Children's Fund study estimated that as many as 200,000 children were trafficked for labor within the region. A survey conducted jointly by the International Labor Organization and the chocolate producers in Côte d'Ivoire the following year estimated that perhaps 5,000 to 10,000 children were used as indentured or slave labor on the country's cocoa plantations; many thousands more were working for family members but subjected to harsh manual labor inappropriate for their age.

Yet, while the boycott drive is well-intentioned (if decidedly unromantic), it is also wrong. It is true that abusive child labor continues to plague cocoa production. But calls for a boycott would harm the very children the activists are trying to help. In truth, the civil war in Côte d'Ivoire is currently a greater obstacle to ending child labor in the chocolate business than any other factor, including the chocolate companies. If consumers really cared about ending child slavery in Côte d'Ivoire, they would direct their protests less at the makers of chocolate turtles and more at Turtle Bay.

Government Is Chaos

In 2001, amid pressure from consumers and international labor groups, the world chocolate industry signed an accord aimed at combating illegal child labor. Under that agreement, known as the Harkin-Engel protocol, chocolate producers pledged to introduce a certification system by 2005 that would guarantee that cocoa had been harvested without using child slaves. But, in September 2002, Côte d'Ivoire plunged into a civil war that has left the country split in two, with the government controlling the south and a rebel coalition controlling the country's north. Since then, a kind of cold peace—with occasionally violent flare-ups—has taken hold. Some 8,000 U.N. peacekeepers and 4,000 French soldiers currently separate the warring parties.

Although actual combat between the two sides has only been sporadic over the past four years, the instability and the de facto partition of the country has hampered any efforts to educate farmers and monitor the cocoa harvest. The International Cocoa Initiative (ICI), the industry-funded foundation that, in accordance with the Harkin-Engel Protocol, is charged with stamping out the worst child labor practices, has managed to launch pilot programs in just six Ivorian communities (compared with 24 pilot programs in Ghana, which is at peace). Also, the chocolate industry had hoped to rely on Ivorian government inspectors to police labor practices on the farms.

But the government has been in such chaos since the war began that few inspectors have been trained—and even those available have not been permitted to work in the rebel-held north. The same goes for representatives of the chocolate industry and a variety of labor rights NGOs [non-governmental organizations]: Their travel to the north has also been restricted due to safety concerns. In October [2007], Peter McAllister, the ICI's executive director, cited Côte d'Ivoire's civil war as a "major hindrance" to developing programs in the country. There's not much the industry can do: It missed its 2005 deadline to create a certification system, and it has negotiated an extension until 2008, by which time it promises to implement monitoring for just half the cocoa-producing areas of Côte d'Ivoire and Ghana.

Reconciliation Depends on New Elections

Until stability returns and Côte d'Ivoire's north and south are reunited, there is little chance that efforts to improve child labor conditions will gain much momentum. But reconciliation remains a long way off. Numerous peace agreements between the government and the rebels, brokered under the auspices of the United Nations, the African Union and the Economic Community of West African States (ECOWAS) have quickly collapsed. The country's president, Laurent Gbagbo, has repeatedly antagonized the opposition by refusing to relinquish key powers to a temporary power-sharing government.

Meanwhile the rebel forces repeatedly have balked at disarmament. Plans for new elections, a key milestone toward rec-

Archbishop of York Calls for Boycott of Chocolate Not Certified as Fairtrade

[On October 30, 2007] the Archbishop [of York, Dr. John Sentamu] launched a "chocolate challenge" ... [and] asked consumers "to buy only Fairtrade chocolate."

He said: "If you can't find it in your favourite shop, ask to see the manager and say that you will only buy goods which are not produced by slave labour. ... If you keep that promise, you could be playing your part in ending a 21st-century iniquity."

Ruth Gledhill,
"If That Chocolate Is Not Fairtrade,
Then Don't Buy It, Says the Archbishop of York,"
Times Online, *October 31, 2007. www.timesonline.co.uk.*

onciliation, have twice been postponed—first from October 2005 to October 2006, and now again to October 2007. Another round of negotiations, sponsored by ECOWAS and aimed at implementing the existing peace agreements, are currently under way in Burkina Faso. (The outgoing head of the U.N. mission to Côte d'Ivoire, the Swedish diplomat Pierre Schori, has warned the two sides: "Don't blow it this time. There won't be any more excuses.")

Already, because of the controversy over child labor and the civil war, Côte d'Ivoire's share of the world cocoa market has fallen.

And, yet, while most of the blame for the ongoing stalemate rests with Gbagbo and rebel leader Guillaume Soro, the United Nations and the members of the Security Council haven't exactly stepped up to the plate. Schori, in an interview with UPI [United Press International Inc.], complained that, when he took over the U.N. mission, he received no recommendations from his predecessor and that the U.N. effort originally lacked urgency.

Chocolate Boycott Not the Answer

Hoping to prove that "African solutions to African problems" can work, the Security Council has tended to take a back seat in any negotiations to ECOWAS and the African Union. The Security Council has since intervened with sticks: It imposed an arms embargo on the country in 2004, and it threatened to ban the travel and seize the assets of key players on both sides if peace talks were not resumed.

[A] boycott on chocolate isn't going to keep children from slavery or fill their stomachs . . . for now, cocoa sales may be one of the few things keeping many Ivorian children from starving.

But carrots—economic aid and security guarantees—could work, and the Security Council has been slow to offer them. The United States in particular has been reluctant to get involved, even though it might be able to serve as an honest broker in a way that Burkina Faso (where the rebels found sanctuary before the abortive 2002 coup that started the civil war) or France (which has been accused of supporting the rebellion and which has the baggage of being the country's former colonial master) cannot. A political settlement—not a chocolate boycott—ought to be the focus for labor and human rights groups, because only with peace can the industry police its farms.

In the near term, a boycott of chocolate would also hurt, not help, many poor Ivorian farmers—and their children. Agriculture accounts for 27 percent of the country's GDP [gross domestic product]. And, while it is true that country's cocoa farmers receive just a fraction of the price a consumer pays for a piece of chocolate (most of the money goes to marketing and processing costs), cocoa sales are still all many farmers have to live on.

Already, because of the controversy over child labor and the civil war, Côte d'Ivoire's share of the world cocoa market has fallen. And the war has badly hurt the country's economy: It has tumbled from 156th to 164th out of the 177 countries ranked by the U.N. Development Program's annual Human Development Index. What's more, fully 45 percent of its population now lives below the poverty line, compared with 30 percent before the civil war began. That includes a lot of children, since it is estimated that 42 percent of the country's 18.5 million inhabitants are younger than 15. That's why responsible children's rights groups, like the Canadian arm of Save the Children, have stopped short of endorsing a chocolate boycott.

Other children's rights advocates should follow suit. It's all well and good to nudge chocolate producers toward better labor practices despite the ongoing conflict. But until peace and stability return to Côte d'Ivoire, a boycott on chocolate isn't going to keep children from slavery or fill their stomachs. (In fact, for now, cocoa sales may be one of the few things keeping many Ivorian children from starving.) But, in at least one respect, Teun van de Keuken, is right: When you bite into the delicious bon bon your lover gave you today, you really should feel guilty—about the calories.

Indian Children Are Exploited in the Handmade Carpet Industry

Charles Jacobs

Charles Jacobs discusses the plight of child carpet slaves in India in the following viewpoint. He describes extremely harsh living conditions and miniscule payments for the child slaves. Jacobs also gives an account of the work being done by Kailash Satyarthi, an activist experienced in loom raids who is on a mission of ending child slavery. Jacobs is the president of the American Anti-Slavery Group, a United States-based organization working to abolish modern-day slavery and supply aid to its victims.

As you read, consider the following questions:

1. How many children does the Bonded Labor Liberation Front believe to be involved in India's handmade woolen carpet industry?
2. In a system of debt bondage, why is it difficult for the original sum to be repaid, as explained by Jacobs?
3. What is the meaning of the RugMark union label?

M ost people believe slavery no longer exists, but it is still very much alive. From Khartoum to Calcutta, from Brazil to Bangladesh, men, women, and children live and work as

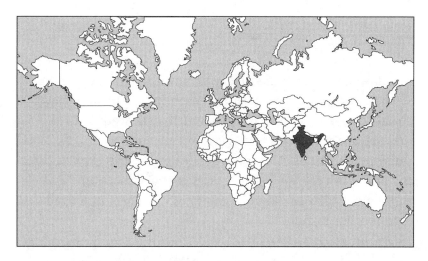

slaves or in slave-like conditions. According to the London-based Anti-Slavery International (ASI), the world's oldest human-rights organization, there are at least 27 million people in bondage. Indeed, there may be more slaves in the world than ever before.

This fact is generally not known. In part, this is because modern-day slavery does not fit our familiar images of shackles, whips, and auctions. Contemporary forms of human bondage include such practices as forced labor, servile marriage, debt bondage, child labor, and forced prostitution. Modern slaves can be concubines, camel jockeys, or cane cutters. They might weave carpets, build roads, or clear forests. Though the vast majority are no longer sold at public auction, today's slaves are often no better off than their more familiar predecessors. Indeed, in many cases, their lives are more brutal and hazardous. . . .

A Stolen Childhood

Five-year-old Santosh was playing with friends in his village in Bahar when a group of men rode up in a jeep and offered to take the children to a movie. Instead, they were driven 400 miles to Allahabad—the heart of India's "carpet belt"—and sold into slavery.

Locked in a room and given no food until he agreed to weave on the looms, Santosh made Oriental carpets for nine years, working from 4:00 in the morning to 11:00 at night, every day, without breaks. He was never given a single rupee [Indian currency] for his labor. When he cut his finger with a sharp tool, the loom master shaved match heads into the cut and set the sulfur on fire. He didn't want the child's blood staining the carpet. After he was rescued, Pharis Harvey, director of the International Labor Rights and Education Fund, described Santosh as "almost catatonic. He had practically no emotion left in him."

Hard numbers are hard to come by, but in India, the Bonded Labor Liberation Front believes that between 200,000 and 300,000 children are involved in the handmade woolen carpet industry, one of the largest export earners for the country. If one includes the 500,000 in Pakistan and 200,000 more in Nepal, the number of Asian child slaves in the carpet industry may reach one million.

Living in Fear

These children work from toddlerhood to adolescence, from dawn to dusk, in horrid conditions. Harvey's group describes the scene: "Children work in damp pits near the loom. Potable water is often unavailable and food consists of a few chapatis [bread balls], onions and salt. Common practice is to keep the children hungry so they will stay awake and work longer hours. The children often are made to sleep on the ground next to their looms, or in nearby sheds. After working from ten to fourteen hours, they are expected to clean out their sheds and set up work for the next day."

Apart from the deep cuts the children suffer on their hands from the weaving tools, the dust and fluff from the wool brings on lung diseases and their eyesight is damaged from close work under poor lighting. And, like Santosh, many have been forcefully separated from their families. Harvey spoke to

---

Indian Children Treated Like Animals

Child laborers and prostitutes exist in such large numbers for a very simple, yet horrific, reason: they are cheap commodities. Children cost less than cattle; a cow or buffalo costs an average 20,000 rupees [Indian currency], but a child can be bought and traded like an animal for 500 to 2,000 rupees. They can be paid the least, exploited the most, and due to their largely invisible status have virtually no power against their oppressors.

While factories in China and Central America that exploit children are often in the news, India is the largest example of a country plagued by this human rights abuse, with the highest number of child laborers in the world.

Shelley Seale,
"Children as Chattel: Child Labor & Trafficking in India,"
The Weight of Silence, *2007. www.stopchildslavery.com.*

---

several children who were kidnapped and later freed after between six and nine years of servitude. Friends who tried to leave were tortured or even killed. Children live in constant fear of the loom masters.

Apart from the deep cuts the children suffer on their hands from the weaving tools, the dust and fluff from the wool brings on lung diseases and their eyesight is damaged from close work under poor lighting.

Kailash Satyarthi rescues child slaves. He was shown on American TV in 1995 leading raids on loom masters. Satyarthi explains that children become carpet slaves in several ways. About 10 percent are kidnapped, simply stolen off the streets like Santosh. Another group may be given over to labor contractors who falsely promise that the children will be educated and cared for while being taught a trade.

Finally, many children are entrapped in a system of debt bondage still widespread in Asia and the subcontinent. From time immemorial, very poor people have pledged their own labor and that of family members as security against a loan taken in a time of crisis. Tragically, the original sum is hardly ever repaid: Because they are mortgaged personally on a 24-hour basis, workers inevitably incur new debts for food, clothing, and shelter. Added to exorbitant interest rates, this ensures families will pass on their ever-mounting debt to their children for generations. People are thus born into slavery. . . .

Hope on the Horizon

In February 1993, a consortium of European and Asian rights groups began the RugMark Campaign, which licenses exporters and manufacturers and affixes the "RugMark"—sort of a union label certifying carpets made without the use of child labor. . . .

According to Harvey, RugMark is an experiment that offers hope. But the problem is daunting. Satyarthi, who pledges his life to end this horror, proclaims that child slavery is "the biggest shame in the world . . . The biggest human-rights violation is child slavery, turning humans into animals."

Satyarthi has faith that as Americans learn of the plight of the slaves, "they will not buy items made from the blood and sweat of children. American taxpayers spend millions on 'development' in poor countries. Why not press governments that receive this aid to institute free and compulsory education for all children?"

Chinese Children Are Kidnapped and Enslaved in Brick Kilns

Congressional-Executive Commission on China

In the following viewpoint, the Congressional-Executive Commission on China reports the trafficking of young children and mentally impaired individuals. Former governor of the Shanxi province, where a great deal of this was taking place, Yu Youjun, apologized for the scandal and vowed to take responsibility. The article discusses the punishments handed out to owners, managers and other Communist Party officials for their role in kidnapping children and mentally impaired individuals and forcing them to work in brick kilns in the Shanxi and Henan provinces.

As you read, consider the following questions:

1. According to the viewpoint, in May and June 2007, how many individuals were enslaved in the Shanxi brick kilns?

2. As stated in the article, about how many hours per day were the children forced to work?

3. What types of punishments did kiln owners and managers receive?

"China Human Rights and Rule of Law Update: Official Defends Response to Forced Labor Scandal," Virtual Academy, May 5, 2008. © 2002–2008 Congressional-Executive Commission on China. All rights reserved. Reproduced by permission.

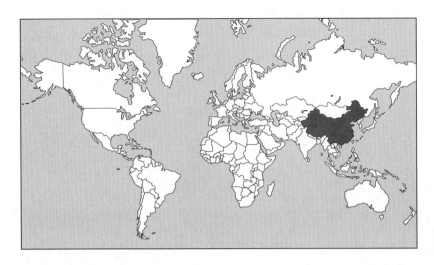

Official Defends Response to Forced Labor Scandal

Yu Youjun, the former provincial governor of Shanxi province, described as "unparalleled" the punishment of 95 local Communist Party officials for their role in a scandal involving the enslavement of more than 1,300 people, including kidnapped children and mentally challenged adults, discovered working in Shanxi brick kilns in May and June 2007. According to an October 22, 2007, *China Daily* article, "About 8 of the 95 officials were expelled from the Party and lost their jobs, 30 were dismissed from their posts and more than 20 officials were demoted." The head of the provincial department of labor and social security and the mayors of Linfen and Yuncheng cities were "required to make a self-criticism at an official conference."

According to the *China Daily*, Yu said that the harshness of the punishments was unprecedented in Shanxi's history. "Officials at county and township levels are mainly responsible for the management of brick kilns and small mines, therefore we focused on them," Yu was quoted as saying. Authorities initially announced the punishments of the 95 officials in July 2007, according to a July 16 *China Daily* article.

Child Labor Abuse in China

Chinese newspapers are constantly peppered with accounts of the death and injury of child laborers, and of disputes that arise because of unusually low wages, or the withholding of pay, with no region of the country exempted. . . .

A 14-year-old boy was killed in an explosion while filling a tank with naphthalene at a chemical factory near Nanjing. A 15-year-old boy was dragged into a cotton gin and crushed to death in Nanchang after working a succession of 20-hour days. And 70 girls from rural Henan Province were brought by their teacher to work at a grape processing plant in Ningbo, where their hands bled from working 16-hour shifts.

Howard W. French,
"Fast-Growing China Says Little of Child Slavery's Role,"
New York Times, *June 21, 2007. www.nytimes.com.*

In July, a death sentence, life imprisonment, and other prison sentences were given to owners, managers, and employees at the kilns, according to a July 17 *China Daily* article. The October report noted that "life and even death sentences were given to five kiln owners, managers and guards."

In June [2007], Yu apologized for the forced labor scandal and said he would take responsibility for it, according to a June 23 *New York Times* report. In September, the State Council appointed Yu as a vice-minister in the national Ministry of Culture, as well as Party chief within the Ministry, according to a September 7, 2007 *Xinhua* article. Yu was also named a Central Committee member at the 17th Chinese Communist Party Congress held in October, as noted on the People's Daily Web site (undated).

As reported in the Congressional-Executive Commission on China 2007 Annual Report (via the Government Printing Office Web site), in May and June 2007, Chinese media and Internet activists uncovered a massive network of forced labor in brick kilns in Shanxi and Henan provinces. Reports indicated that people forced to work in the kilns included children and mentally challenged adults kidnapped by human traffickers and sold to the kilns, where they were beaten, denied food, and forced to work up to 20 hours per day.

Pakistani Children Enslaved as Camel Jockeys

IRIN (Integrated Regional Information Network)

The following IRIN (Integrated Regional Information Network) report investigates a form of child slavery in Pakistan, where small boys—most between four and eight years old—were sold by their families and forced to work as jockeys in the camel racing industry. Though banned in 2005 in the United Arab Emirates (UAE), officials believe there are still many challenges ahead in putting an end to the practice. A government initiative, supported by the United Nations Children's Fund (UNICEF), is now working to return former child jockeys to their families and provide rehabilitation. Many former victims, however, are finding it difficult to adjust after being abused and traumatized.

As you read, consider the following questions:

1. Approximately how many children have returned home under the UNICEF-supported government initiative?
2. What will happen if parents attempt to sell their children back into slavery after they have been returned home?
3. What is the Community Action Plan, being carried out by UNICEF, accomplishing within communities?

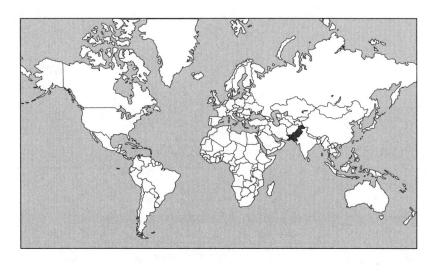

Every morning, Aziz, 12, cycles to school, his satchel bal-
anced carefully over the handlebars. His life has changed
dramatically over the past year and the former camel jockey,
who spent five years in the Gulf until his return in 2005, is
beginning to adapt to a different way of life.

"I will never forget the camels and being strapped onto
those beasts. But I now hope I can put that behind me, get an
education and go on to work in an office," Aziz said in his village near the southern Punjab town of Muzaffargarh.

Muzaffargarh district, with a population of around 3 million, is among the poorest districts of Pakistan's populous
Punjab province. Over the years, families from southern Punjab, as well as neighbouring Sindh province, have sold small
boys, most aged between four and eight years, for use as camel
jockeys in the United Arab Emirates (UAE) and other Gulf
countries, where the sport remains a popular pastime.

The children are used because they are light, which allows
the camel to run faster. Their screams of terror spur on the
animal. The children are deliberately underfed to keep down
their weight, and many have suffered terrible injuries after
falling off the camels.

The use of the child camel jockeys, usually bought from their parents or other relatives for around US $1,500, was banned in the UAE under a new law passed in May 2005, with violators facing jail terms of up to three years and/or a fine of almost $14,000.

> *The children are used because they are light, which allows the camel to run faster. . . . The children are deliberately underfed to keep down their weight.*

Since then, under a Pakistan government initiative supported by the United Nations Children's Fund (UNICEF), at least 600 former child jockeys have returned home. Others have been repatriated to Bangladesh or Sudan, the two other home countries of the jockeys.

Most are now back with their families, with some of the parents claiming they had no idea that the children would be used as jockeys.

"We thought they would be given jobs and would gain an opportunity to escape misery and poverty here," said Muhammad Khurram, an uncle of one of the boys sent to the UAE from Muzaffargarh.

All the families selling the children, in exchange for either a lump sum or monthly payment of the children's 'salaries' are extremely poor—often with six, seven or eight other children at home.

The return of a child from the Gulf, in some cases after five or more years away, is not easy to adjust to for either party.

The Lahore-based Child Welfare Protection Bureau (CWPB), run by the Punjab government, has been engaged from the start to receive and rehabilitate the returning children. It continues to keep a close watch on the situation of those who have returned.

According to data maintained by the CWPB, 227 children have returned to their homes in Rahimyar Khan, 131 to Muzaffargarh, 18 to Multan, 50 to Dera Ghazi Khan, and the rest to other areas in the southern Punjab or the neighbouring province of Sindh. Six of the children remain at the CWPB, which has facilities to house over 200 children. Efforts continue to trace their parents, but Dr. Faiza Asghar, who heads the centre, explained, "these children were very young when they were sent to the Gulf. They have no idea who their parents are, or where they formerly lived. We will keep them until they are at least 18, and of course provide for their education, if their families cannot be tracked down."

Today, the six boys at the CWPB don smart uniforms for school and at the centre's playground, smile broadly and confidently at the cameras—a change from the terrified expressions many child camel jockey victims wore when they first returned home in 2005.

In other cases, DNA testing has been used to reunite families. Parents taking back children have also frequently been warned of criminal action should they attempt to sell off their children again. Sixty people involved in human trafficking have, according to official figures, been arrested and are being tried under the relevant laws.

"We are continuing to monitor most of the children who have returned, including the 325 brought back by the CWPB who are now with their families," Asghar explained. Some children had considerable difficulty in adapting to the environment they had left behind before going to the Gulf, and were traumatised by their harsh experiences there, she added.

"Each case is different. Some of the children are still undergoing psychological treatment and facing problems, while others are not," the doctor said.

In some cases, the relatives of former jockeys interviewed by IRIN stated that the children seemed "distant and resentful" and were unwilling to attend school or perform house-

Thousands of Former Child Camel Jockeys to Receive Payouts

A senior Ministry of Interior delegation left for Pakistan yesterday [May 3, 2008], marking the start of an undertaking to track down and compensate the former jockeys. . . .

[T]he jockeys will receive a minimum of US$1,000 . . .

Those who sustained injuries while riding will receive larger amounts, while families of boys who died will also receive compensation. . . .

The compensation scheme is the government's latest effort to reform the sport and address past abuses.

Matt Bradley, "UAE to Give Child Jockeys Payouts,"
The National, May 4, 2008. www.thenational.ae.

hold chores. In fact, some of these children aged six or seven years when they left, returned as angry, embittered teenagers—with siblings or parents in some cases not pleased to have them back in cramped family homes, where food and resources were already scarce.

[S]ome of these children aged six or seven years when they left, returned as angry, embittered teenagers—with siblings or parents in some cases not pleased to have them back in cramped family homes, where food and resources were already scarce.

A Community Action Plan (CAP) to create awareness about the trafficking of children, and to aid the rehabilitation of former camel jockeys, is being carried out by UNICEF, in cooperation with the CWPB and its sub-office in Rahimyar Khan.

The programme includes the education of children, and focuses on providing health care facilities, micro-financing, safe water, and social uplift schemes within communities.

On 18 December 2006, UNICEF welcomed the allocation of US $9 million by the UAE government to assist former camel jockeys who have returned home to their communities.

The UAE also agreed to extend until May 2009 its partnership with UNICEF to assist in the repatriation and rehabilitation of child camel jockeys.

Almost all the children now resettled in the Punjab are back at school. Six hundred bicycles have been provided to returning children by the CWPB to enable them to reach schools, help them resume something resembling normal life, and gain an education that could in the future help them to lead normal lives.

However, officials at the CWPB warned that some of the children—estimated at around 20 percent of those who have returned—continue to face difficulties adjusting to life in their homes and at school, and therefore are not able to attend classes every day.

A few of the older children are also being given vocational training, and organisations in Pakistan are continuing efforts to secure employment for the former jockeys in the UAE.

But despite these efforts, the challenges are far from over. Two weeks ago, Pakistan's Minister of State for Information, Tariq Azeem, stated that there had been a recent attempt to take three children back to the Gulf for camel races, and that these children had been brought back with the cooperation of the UAE authorities.

He promised that the Pakistani government would "continue to pursue" this humanitarian matter at all costs.

Meanwhile, the Karachi-based Ansar Burney Trust, which has also been closely involved with the effort to repatriate and rehabilitate the child camel jockeys, is also continuing efforts to locate those that still remain in the Gulf.

"An intensive search and identification of underage jockeys is continuing," Ansar Burney, the group's chairman, said recently.

But while the efforts of governments and welfare organisations have helped highlight the issue, bring about necessary changes in law to end the use of children as jockeys and undertake rehabilitation efforts, the socio-economic issues which underpin such abuse of children remain in place.

"Families are so poor, they barely survive. In despair they take desperate measures, including the sale of children. Until this issue of deprivation is addressed, there can be no guarantee more children will not be trafficked to the Gulf or elsewhere, either as jockeys or for other kinds of slave labour," said Abbas Akhtar, a Multan-based social activist who has closely followed the issue of the child camel jockeys, and the difficult task of giving the returning children the childhood they missed out on while on the camel racing tracks of the Middle East.

African Children and Infants Sold by Parents Become Slaves in the United Kingdom

David Harrison

In the following viewpoint, journalist David Harrison explores the disturbing illicit trade of African children, many who are infants, sold by their parents and trafficked into the United Kingdom (UK). Parents suffering from extreme poverty in Africa are deceived by traffickers and led to believe that their children will have better opportunities in the UK. In 2006, Harrison won the distinguished Paul Foot Award for his investigation of sex trafficking in Eastern Europe; his work was praised by the United Nations and helped elicit action from the Home Office, the government department for immigration and passports, drug policy, counter-terrorism, and police.

As you read, consider the following questions:

1. Apart from being used as domestic slaves, how are the children being used for fraud?
2. As cited in the article, according to the recent survey by the government's Child Exploitation and Online Protection Centre, how many children had been trafficked to Britain?

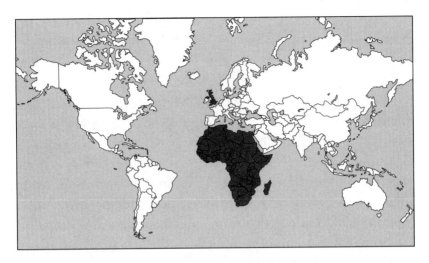

3. After the children grow older and their owners no longer have any use for them, what often becomes of them?

Hundreds of young children are being sold and "trafficked" to Britain from Africa to be exploited as modern-day slaves, it can be revealed.

The illicit trade in children—sold by their parents, some while still babies, to criminal gangs and people traffickers—has been uncovered by a *Sunday Telegraph* investigation.

An undercover reporter was offered several children for sale by their parents in Nigeria: two boys aged three and five for £5,000, [British pounds] or £2,500 for one, and a 10-month-old baby for £2,000. Teenage girls—including some still pregnant—were willing to sell their babies for less than £1,000.

Teenage girls—including some still pregnant—were willing to sell their babies for less than £1,000.

One international trafficker, tracked down in Lagos, claimed to be buying up to 500 children a year.

Impoverished African parents are being lured by the traffickers' promises of "a better life" for their children, thousands of miles away in cities including London, Birmingham and Manchester.

But, once brought to Britain, the children are used as a fraudulent means to obtain illicit housing and other welfare benefits, totaling tens of thousands of pounds each a year.

From the age of seven, rather than being sent to school, they are exploited as domestic slaves, forced to work for up to 18 hours a day, cleaning, cooking and looking after other younger children, or put to work in restaurants and shops.

Some of the children are also subjected to physical and sexual abuse, while others even find themselves accused of being witches and become victims of exorcism rites in "traditional" African churches in Britain.

Child Trafficking Is "Totally Unacceptable"

Campaigners called last night [January 28, 2008] for the Government and the police to take "urgent action" to end this "21st century child slavery".

"These children are being abused under our noses in our own country," said Chris Beddoe, the director of End Child Prostitution and Trafficking, a British-based coalition of international charities.

"It is totally unacceptable. We need urgent action to identify these children as they enter the UK [United Kingdom], find those who are being abused and offer proper protection to those who escape or are freed from their abusers."

Vernon Coaker, the Home Office minister responsible for the prevention of trafficking, described child traffickers as "evil" and said anybody who could buy and sell babies was "sick".

But David Davis, the Conservative shadow home secretary, said: "The Government has utterly failed to take decisive action to tackle human trafficking.

How Are Children Brought to the UK?

Any port of entry into the UK [United Kingdom] might be used by traffickers. There is evidence that some children are trafficked via numerous transit countries and many may travel through other European Union countries before arriving in the UK.

Recent experience suggests that as checks have improved at the larger ports of entry such as Heathrow and Gatwick airports, traffickers are starting to use smaller ports, as well as other regional airports. Traffickers are also known to use the Eurostar rail service and ferries to UK sea ports. . . .

A number of children arrive in the UK accompanied by adults who are either not related to them or in circumstances which raise child protection concerns. For example, there may be little evidence of any pre-existing relationship or even an absence of any knowledge of the sponsor. There may be unsatisfactory accommodation arranged in the UK, or perhaps no evidence of parental permission for the child to travel to the UK or stay with the sponsor. These irregularities may be the only indication that the child could be a victim of trafficking.

"Working Together to Safeguard Children—
Safeguarding Children Who May Have Been Trafficked,"
HM Government, UK Department for Children,
Schools and Families, 2007. www.dcsf.gov.uk.

"A Conservative government would take a range of practical measures—developed in detail over the last two years—to curb all aspects of this evil trade, which threatens Britain and the most vulnerable in our society."

A recent survey by the Government's Child Exploitation and Online Protection Centre claimed that 330 children, including 14 aged under 12, many of them from Africa, had been trafficked to Britain over the past year.

The police and campaigners believe, however, that this is just the "tip of the iceberg" and that the true figure is likely to be in the thousands.

The *Sunday Telegraph* can reveal how the trade starts more than three thousand miles away in Africa where babies are sold to predatory traffickers, able to persuade desperately poor and often illiterate parents to hand over their children. The children are then sold, at high profit, as "home helps" to African families in Britain and in other European and North American cities.

The traffickers use a network of corrupt officials and co-traffickers to obtain passports and visas, often giving the children new names.

Many of the young victims are flown directly from Lagos in Nigeria to London's airports. Others are taken, via other west African states such as Ghana and Benin, to "transit" cities, including Paris.

A growing number of the African slave children arrives in Britain unaccompanied, as asylum-seekers, or with "private foster parents".

Children Falling Through Cracks in a Flawed System

Debbie Ariyo, the executive director of the London-based charity Africans Unite Against Child Abuse, said: "This trade is a disgrace. These children are not going to loving homes.

"They are being cynically used by adults as slave labour and to defraud the state and then when they get older and have served their purpose and no longer attract entitled to benefits they are thrown out on to the streets with no papers even to prove who they are. These are damaged, traumatised children and we have to end this misery."

Campaigners said that many of the slave children—psychologically and often physically damaged at 18—were thrown out of the houses of their "owners".

They are left to fend for themselves, usually with no papers or documents to prove who they are. With nowhere to turn, many fall into crime and the sex trade. Those that come to the attention of the authorities when they commit a crime or go to social services for help are usually brusquely deported as illegal immigrants.

The Government will unveil new measures next month aimed at giving more protection to victims of child trafficking.

Mr. Coaker said: "We have tightened our visa requirements and our ports of entry and we are gathering intelligence to help us stop this horrific trade."

A senior Scotland Yard officer said: "The traffickers and the people who buy the children and use them as domestic slaves have no regard for their well-being and we are determined to catch those involved in this vile business.

"But this is a hidden crime, going on largely in Britain's African communities and we would urge people in those communities to contact us if they suspect that any child in their area is being abused. We need their co-operation. They must not turn a blind eye."

Godwin Morka, the executive director of Lagos's anti-trafficking unit, Nathip, admitted that child trafficking was "rampant" in many Nigerian states. "We know these children are not going to happy homes and we are doing what we can on limited resources."

Haiti's Child Slaves Suffer Abuse in "Restavek" System

Pete Pattisson

Although the "restavek"—meaning "stay with"—system of child domestic work is legal in Haiti, restavek children living with families have been found suffering from mental, physical, and sexual abuse. According to writer Pete Pattisson, the Haitian government has done little to address the problem, leaving charities to help save and rehabilitate restavek children. Pattisson is a widely published, award-winning photojournalist who has worked with non-governmental organizations, including Anti-Slavery International. Pattisson is currently working on an extensive project documenting modern-day forms of slavery across the globe.

As you read, consider the following questions:

1. What are restavek children supposed to receive in exchange for domestic work?

2. What percentage of child domestics are girls, according to the article?

3. What is the Foyer Maurice Sixto organization doing to help child domestics in Haiti?

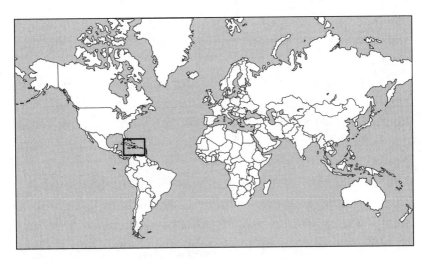

In the first country to rid itself of colonial slavery, a modern form of slavery is flourishing. Thedna Pierre, a 15-year-old girl who works for a woman in Haiti's capital, Port-au-Prince, has the scars to prove it.

"She bites me, she burns me, she beats me," she said, seething with anger. "One time her baby son spat in my face, so I smacked him lightly on the hand. She went crazy. She grabbed the spoon she was cooking with and thrashed me with it. The spoon was burning hot and now I have these scars on my legs. Living with her is like living in hell."

Thedna is a "restavek", one of the former French colony's 300,000 child domestic chattels. In a tradition that dates back to the slave trade, poor Haitian children are sent from the countryside to work for families in the cities, typically from the age of eight or nine, but sometimes from as young as five.

[F]amilies are often unable, or unwilling, to pay to the children's education, and instead force them to work up to 18 hours a day.

There is an expectation that they will be sent to school in return for their labour. But, while this may have happened in the past, today wealthy Haitians prefer to employ maids, and restaveks work for families who are only a little better off than their own.

Such families are often unable, or unwilling, to pay for the children's education, and instead force them to work up to 18 hours a day. Modern-day restaveks—the word is derived from the French rester avec, or "stay with"—simply exchange rural poverty for urban serfdom.

The practice has been condemned by the London-based charity Anti-Slavery International, which is campaigning to stamp out modern forms of slavery—particularly involving children—in the run-up to next month's [March 2007's] 200th anniversary of the abolition of the slave trade.

"The restavek system is one of the most severe examples of child domestic work, both in terms of the children's young age and the abuses they suffer," said the organisation's director, Aidan McQuade. "These children are hidden from view, making them particularly vulnerable to physical, mental and sexual abuse."

Restavek System Not Illegal

Many Haitians see it differently. The small Caribbean nation, which became independent in 1804 after a slave revolt led by Toussaint L'Ouverture, prides itself as the first to throw off the yoke of colonial slavery, and few regard the restavek system as comparable.

Marie Anne Hera keeps two child domestics in a shack on the slopes above the capital. "I'm not taking care of them the way I should," she said, "but it's not my fault. I just don't have enough money."

She treats her restaveks very differently to her own children. "She sends her own children to school, but I have to stay here and work," complained Micheleine, 14, one of the restaveks. "They get to eat rice and I am fed corn. They sleep on the bed, but I sleep on the floor."

Haitians Justify Restavèk System

Today in Haiti, an estimated one out of every ten children is a *restavèk*. . . .

Haitians have done very little over the years to eliminate the *restavèk* system. Most activists do not see the *restavèk* system as a serious obstacle to developing a human rights culture. In particular, respect for the basic rights of the child is not seen as an obstacle to efforts aimed at developing better overall human relations and patterns of behavior. Rather than being seen as a single factor that influences the *restavèk* system, poverty continues to be used as a pretext to justify its acceptance and the corresponding lack of sustained effort to abolish it—particularly since simple economic solutions are not forthcoming.

National Coalition for Haitian Rights,
"Restavèk No More: Eliminating Child Slavery in Haiti,"
Executive Summary, 2007. www.nchr.org.

Although the restavek system is not illegal, those who work with its victims do not hesitate to brand it slavery. Marline Mondesir, the director of a local organisation which supports child domestics said: "These children are slaves, because they are the first to wake in the morning and the last to go to bed.

They get beaten up and there's nobody to speak up for them. One child we helped had his head cut open with a machete, another had her back slashed with a razor blade, another was burned with hot oil and another had his arm broken."

Many are beaten with stiff cowhide whips, known as rigoises, which are designed for use on children and are widely available in shops. More than 70 percent of child domestics are girls and sexual abuse is so common that restaveks are said to be "la pou sa"—"there for that".

Children Are Like Zombies

Evelyne Joseph, 15, was brought to Port-au-Prince by her uncle after her mother died. When he could no longer afford to pay for her schooling, he sent her to work for another family. She was only 10. Evelyne said: "One day last year, when I was alone in the house, a guy who lived next door raped me. I got pregnant and the family kicked me out."

Evelyne moved back in with her uncle. "I was determined to have the child. I knew something good would come out of it," she said, cradling her eight-month-old daughter, Vickencia. "I just hope someone will pay for me to go back to school."

Stephanie George, 12, works from 5am to 11pm every day. "I don't get any rest or days off," she said. "The only time I get to rest is when I fall asleep. In the future I would like to go back to the countryside, to my parents. I haven't heard from them since I left."

The issue is largely unaddressed by the Haitian government, whose president, René Préval, was elected last February after two years of near anarchy. Despite the backing of an 8,000-strong United Nations force, the authorities can barely keep law and order, leaving charities to grapple with the problem.

The Foyer Maurice Sixto runs schools and camps for child domestics, to give them the chance to be children again—a process that Wenes Geanty, the director, describes as "de-zombification". He said: "These children behave like zombies because they can't communicate. They can only obey. We try to make these children know they are as human as anyone else."

Periodical Bibliography

The following articles have been selected to supplement the diverse views presented in this chapter.

Associated Press — "Child 'Slavery' Now Being Imported to U.S.," MSNBC, December 29, 2008. www.msnbc.msn.com.

Peter Conradi — "Kidnapped Children Starve as Camel Jockey Slaves," *The Sunday Times*, March 27, 2005. www.timesonline.co.uk.

Gilbert da Costa — "Nigeria Intercepts 62 Suspected Child Laborers," VOA (Voice Of America) News, July 18, 2007. www.voanews.com.

Sophie Goodchild and Jonathan Thompson — "5,000 Child Sex Slaves in UK," *The Independent* (UK), February 25, 2007. www.independent.co.uk.

Dan Harris — "82-Year-Old American Woman Frees Child Slaves in Nepal," ABC News, July 6, 2008. http://abcnews.go.com.

Carol Nader — "Women Tricked into Selling Unborn into Slavery," *The Age* (Melbourne, Australia), August 5, 2008.

Rageh Omaar — "The World of Modern Child Slavery," BBC, March 27, 2007. http://news.bbc.co.uk.

Dan Rivers — "Girl, 6, Embodies Cambodia's Sex Industry," CNN, January 26, 2007. www.cnn.com.

Kalpana Sharma — "Making Visible the Invisible," *The Hindu*, January 11, 2009. www.hindu.com.

Sami Yousafzai and Ron Moreau — "The Opium Brides of Afghanistan," *Newsweek*, April 7, 2008. www.newsweek.com.

For Further Discussion

Chapter 1

1. Many of the authors in the first chapter point out that apologies for slavery have been futile—and even damaging in some cases. Why do you think leaders around the world believe that it is important to apologize for past slavery injustices? Why are their apologies being received with mixed emotions? According to many of the viewpoints, what productive steps can be made beyond apologies? In considering the Caribbean "Sites of Memory on the Slave Route" project, what other kinds of positive contributions do you think countries could make to deal with the legacy of slavery?

2. Some of the material in this chapter touches upon the controversial issue of slavery reparations. Darcus Howe argues that reparations to Africans are warranted since the continent continues to suffer from slave trade consequences today, while Peter Flaherty and John Carlisle make a strong case against slave reparations in America. After reading the viewpoints in this chapter, do you think that financial reparations for slavery should be made? Do you think that that the descendents of African slaves in America ought to receive reparations? Why or why not?

Chapter 2

1. After considering the viewpoints in this chapter, why do you think modern-day slavery has become so widespread? Why do you think many people are not aware that slavery still exists today? How is modern-day slavery different from slavery in the past? Why is trafficking in persons so difficult to identify and prosecute in many countries?

2. The U.S. Department of State defines severe forms of human trafficking and then treats specific kinds, such as forced labor, bonded labor, involuntary domestic servitude, child labor, sexual exploitation, and child soldiers. Since a person does not need to be physically transported from one location to another in order to become a victim, which forms of forced servitude might be be carried out in the area where you live? How might this be accomplished? How could you and your community discover and rescue possible victims?

Chapter 3

1. After considering the viewpoints in this chapter, what are some of the physical, emotional, and social consequences sex trafficking victims face in captivity and thereafter?

2. Though governments and NGOs (non-governmental organizations) are working to fight sex trafficking, it has become pervasive in many parts of the world. What are some obstacles preventing the assistance of victims and prosecution of traffickers? Do you agree with Joel Brinkley that confusing prostitution with slavery is hindering efforts to fight trafficking? Why or why not?

Chapter 4

1. After reading the viewpoints in this chapter, consider the relationship between poverty and child slavery. Many parents are deceived by traffickers, believing that their children will escape poverty by being sold. What do you think can be done to make parents less vulnerable to traffickers?

2. What are some of the physical, emotional, and social consequences exploited children face? What do you think can be done to increase awareness?

Organizations to Contact

American Anti-Slavery Group (AASG)
198 Tremont Street #421, Boston, MA   02116
(617) 426-8161 • fax: (270) 964-2716
Web site: www.iabolish.org

The American Anti-Slavery Group (AASG) was founded by
Dr. Charles Jacobs. A nonprofit organization, the AASG is
dedicated to abolishing modern-day slavery, as well as supporting and empowering survivors. The organization's primary concentration is on systems of chattel slavery in Sudan
and Mauritania. The AASG has four areas of focus: creating
awareness, carrying out advocacy, engaging in activism, and
providing direct aid for victims. The organization's Web site
features a blog. Other online educational resources are available, including a collection of essays.

Anti-Slavery International
Thomas Clarkson House, London   SW9 9TL
   United Kingdom
44-02075018920 • fax: 44-02077384110
e-mail: info@antislavery.org
Web site: www.antislavery.org

Founded in 1839, Anti-Slavery International is known as the
world's oldest international human rights organization. Based
in the United Kingdom, Anti-Slavery International works at
local, national, and international levels to help bring an end to
slavery and its related abuses around the world. The organization is focused on lobbying governments and intergovernmen-
tal agencies, leading campaigns, raising public awareness, supporting and promoting research, and providing valuable
educational resources. Anti-Slavery International houses a library in London, where visitors are welcome to explore an extensive collection of materials, including books, periodicals,

reports, videos, photos, and exhibitions. A variety of educational materials and documents are also available on the organization's Web site. Anti-Slavery International publishes a quarterly magazine, the *Reporter*, which is available to members free of charge.

Canadian Aid for Southern Sudan (CASS)

35 Bruce Street, London, Ontario   N6C 1G5
  Canada
(519) 679-1429 • fax: (519) 439-4170
e-mail: cass.can@sympatico.ca
Web site: www.web.net/cass

Canadian Aid for Southern Sudan (CASS) is a human rights and development organization working to help the people of Sudan who have suffered decades of war. The organization is dedicated to abolishing slavery, helping the people of southern Sudan rebuild their lives and communities, promoting human rights, rehabilitating child soldiers, and building schools. CASS publishes a newsletter, which is available online. Other information can be found on the CASS Web site, including stories documenting the organization's work, and other educational pamphlets.

Coalition to Abolish Slavery & Trafficking (CAST)

5042 Wilshire Boulevard #586, Los Angeles, CA   90036
(213) 365-1906 • fax: (213) 365-5257
e-mail: info@castla.org
Web site: www.castla.org

Established in 1998, the Los Angeles-based Coalition to Abolish Slavery & Trafficking (CAST) assists victims of trafficking and slavery, and works to end such human rights violations. CAST carries out policy advocacy, outreach, public education, and leadership development. A grantee of the Department of Justice and the Department of Health and Human Services, CAST has provided training and technical assistance to thousands of non-governmental organizations and government personnel. The coalition also opened the first shelter for trafficked women in the United States. The CAST Web site offers news and educational resources.

Development and Education Program for Daughters and Communities (DEPDC)

PO Box 10, Mae Sai, Chiang Rai   57130
  Thailand
66-053733186 • fax: 66-053642415
e-mail: info@depdc.org
Web site: www.depdc.org

The Development and Education Program for Daughters and Communities (DEPDC) is a community-based, non-governmental organization in Thailand that works to prevent the trafficking of women and children into the sex industry, as well as exploitative child labor situations. DEPDC offers free education and vocational training, as well as full-time accommodation for children. The organization publishes newsletters, available in PDF format on its Web site. Other resources available on the DEPDC site, include fact sheets, reports, brochures, and a photo gallery.

Free The Slaves (FTS)

514 Tenth Street NW 7th Floor, Washington, DC   20004
(202) 638-1865
e-mail: info@freetheslaves.net
Web site: www.freetheslaves.net

Free the Slaves (FTS) is a nonprofit organization formed in 2000, co-founded by Kevin Bales, author of the award-winning book *Disposable People*, along with Jolene Smith and Peggy Callahan. A research-oriented organization, FTS works with governments to establish anti-slavery laws, recruits businesses to eliminate slavery from their product chains, and educates consumers about slavery. The FTS Web site offers a wealth of information for educational purposes, including online videos, research, publications, and other downloadable materials for students and teachers, such as education packs for classroom use.

The Helen Bamber Foundation
5 Museum House, London WC1A 1JT
  United Kingdom
44-02076314492 • fax: 44-02076314493
e-mail: info@helenbamber.org
Web site: www.helenbamber.org

Based in the United Kingdom, The Helen Bamber Foundation was established in 2005. The organization works to support survivors of gross human rights violations, such as human trafficking for forced labor or prostitution. The foundation is focused on helping survivors rebuild their lives and their self-esteem through social well-being and integration, mind and body therapies, rehabilitation therapies, and health care. The organization is also focused on building awareness through advocacy and education. The organization's Web site offers information on trafficking and a collection of case studies.

Jean R. Cadet Restavec Foundation
11160 Kenwood Road, Cincinnati, OH 45242
Web site: www.restavecfreedom.org

The Jean R. Cadet Restavec Foundation is a nonprofit, non-governmental organization working to bring an end to child slavery in Haiti. The foundation is dedicated to increasing global awareness and providing relief to children trapped in the restavec system. The foundation works to build relationships with the families who keep restavec children and acts as an advocate for them. They also help reunite restavec children with their original families when appropriate. The organization is focused on facility development and educating communities to prevent children from being sent into servitude. Jean R. Cadet is the author of *Restavec: From Haitian Slave Child to Middle-Class American*; proceeds from the book go directly to the Jean R. Cadet Restavec Freedom Foundation. The organization publishes newsletters, available online, as well as a variety of educational materials, including facts, statistics, articles, and online photos and video clips.

La Strada International (LSI)
De Wittenstraat 25, Amsterdam   1052 AK
  The Netherlands
31-0206881414 • fax: 31-0206881013
e-mail: info@lastradainternational.org
Web site: www.lastradainternational.org

La Strada International (LSI) is comprised of nine member organizations from the Netherlands, Poland, the Czech Republic, Ukraine, Bulgaria, Belarus, Bosnia-Herzegovina, Moldova, and Macedonia. All La Strada International member organizations are registered as independent non-governmental organizations. LSI works to prevent trafficking human beings, primarily focusing on women in Central and Eastern Europe. The association publishes a quarterly newsletter, and an extensive collection of news and information is available on its Web site. The LSI online "Documentation Centre" provides a searchable repository of information on trafficking, including many downloadable PDF documents.

National Underground Railroad Freedom Center
50 East Freedom Way, Cincinnati, Ohio   45202
(513) 333-7500
Web site: www.freedomcenter.org

Located on the banks of the Ohio River in downtown Cincinnati, Ohio, the National Underground Railroad Freedom Center opened in 2004. The museum's frame of reference is the story of the underground railroad and America's battle with slavery, but the center also focuses on global modern-day slavery as well. In addition to five permanent exhibitions, many changing exhibits, programs, and activities are presented throughout the year. The center's Web site features an extensive collection of information about the underground railroad in the United States and modern-day slavery around the world, as well as educational resources for teachers.

Polaris Project

PO Box 77892, Washington, DC   20013
(202) 745-1001 • fax: (202) 745-1119
e-mail: info@polarisproject.org
Web site: www.polarisproject.org

Founded in 2002 by Katherine Chon and Derek Ellerman while they were seniors at Brown University, the Polaris Project is one of the largest anti-trafficking organizations in the United States and Japan today. The Polaris Project works to fight human trafficking through direct outreach and victim identification and provides social services and transitional housing to victims. The organization also operates the National Human Trafficking Resource Center (NHTRC), serving as the central national hotline on human trafficking. The Polaris Project works to promote better anti-trafficking legislation and community involvement. The organization's media-rich Web site contains information on recognizing trafficking and understanding slavery, as well as many educational resources, including online video clips.

United Nations Office on Drugs & Crime (UNODC)

PO Box 500, Vienna   1400
   Austria
43-1260605687 • fax: 43-1260605983
e-mail: ahtu@unodc.org
Web site: www.unodc.org

The United Nations Office on Drugs & Crime (UNODC) assists states in drafting laws and creating national anti-trafficking strategies, as well as helping with resources to implement them. The UNODC is the custodian of the Protocol to Prevent, Suppress, and Punish Trafficking in Persons, Especially Women and Children, adopted by the United Nations General Assembly in 2000. The UNODC's anti-trafficking work is focused on trafficking prevention, victim protection, and prosecution of trafficking offenders. The UNODC publishes *Toolkit to Combat Trafficking in Persons*; in addition, the

UNODC Web site offers an extensive collection of information on trafficking, including reports, papers, and leaflets—most available in PDF format.

Bibliography of Books

Adel S. Abadeer — *The Entrapment of the Poor into Involuntary Labor: Understanding the Worldwide Practice of Modern-Day Slavery*. Lewiston: Edwin Mellen Press, 2008.

Alexis A. Aronowitz — *Human Trafficking, Human Misery: The Global Trade in Human Beings*. Westport, CT: Praeger, 2009.

Anne C. Bailey — *African Voices of the Atlantic Slave Trade: Beyond the Silence and the Shame*. Boston, MA: Beacon Press, 2005.

Charlotte Baker and Jennifer Jahn, eds. — *Postcolonial Slavery: An Overview of Colonialism's Legacy*. Newcastle: Cambridge Scholars, 2009.

Kevin Bales — *Disposable People: New Slavery in the Global Economy*. Berkeley and Los Angeles, CA: University of California Press, 1999.

Kevin Bales — *Ending Slavery: How We Free Today's Slaves*. Berkeley and Los Angeles, CA: University of California Press, 2007.

Kevin Bales — *Understanding Global Slavery: A Reader*. Berkeley and Los Angeles, CA: University of California Press, 2005.

David Batstone — *Not for Sale: The Return of the Global Slave Trade—And How We Can Fight It.* New York, NY: HarperCollins, 2007.

Raymond Bechard — *Unspeakable: The Hidden Truth Behind the World's Fastest Growing Crime.* New York, NY: Compel Publishing, 2006.

Douglas A. Blackmon — *Slavery by Another Name: The Reenslavement of Black Americans from the Civil War to World War II.* New York, NY: Doubleday, 2008.

John Bowe — *Nobodies: Modern American Slave Labor and the Dark Side of the New Global Economy.* New York, NY: Random House, 2007.

Alfred L. Brophy — *Reparations: Pro and Con.* New York, NY: Oxford University Press, Inc., 2006.

Jean-Robert Cadet — *Restavec: From Haitian Slave Child to Middle-Class American.* Austin, TX: University of Texas Press, 1998.

David Brion Davis — *Inhuman Bondage: The Rise and Fall of Slavery in the New World.* New York, NY: Oxford University Press, Inc., 2006.

Anthony M. DeStefano — *The War on Human Trafficking: U.S. Policy Assessed.* New Brunswick, NJ: Rutgers University Press, 2008.

Barbara Ehrenreich and Arlie Russell Hochschild	*Global Woman: Nannies, Maids, and Sex Workers in the New Economy.* New York, NY: Metropolitan Books, 2002.
Igor Davor Gaon and Nancy Forbord	*For Sale: Women and Children: Trafficking and Forced Prostitution in Southeast Europe.* Victoria, BC: Trafford, 2005.
Siddharth Kara	*Sex Trafficking: Inside the Business of Modern Slavery.* New York, NY: Columbia University Press, 2009.
Craig Kielburger, with Kevin Major	*Free the Children: A Young Man's Personal Crusade Against Child Labor.* New York, NY: HarperCollins, 1998.
Gilbert King	*Woman, Child for Sale: The New Slave Trade in the 21st Century.* New York, NY: Chamberlain Bros., 2004.
Victor Malarek	*The Natashas: Inside the New Global Sex Trade.* New York, NY: Arcade Publishing, 2004.
Michael T. Martin and Marilyn Yaquinto, eds.	*Redress for Historical Injustices in the United States: On Reparations for Slavery, Jim Crow, and Their Legacies.* Durham, NC: Duke University Press, 2007.
Patricia McCormick	*Sold.* New York, NY: Hyperion, 2006.
Craig McGill	*Human Traffic: Sex, Slaves and Immigration.* London: Vision Paperbacks, 2003.

Catherine Paris	*Modern Day Slavery: Human Trafficking Revealed.* Ocala, FL: Claddagh Ltd. Publishing, 2007.
Toby Shelley	*Exploited: Migrant Labour in the New Global Economy.* New York, NY: Zed Books, 2007.
E. Benjamin Skinner	*A Crime So Monstrous.* New York, NY: Free Press, 2008.
Christien van den Anker	*The Political Economy of New Slavery.* Houndmills, Basingstoke, Hampshire; New York, NY: Palgrave Macmillan, 2004.
James Walvin	*A Short History of Slavery.* London: Penguin, 2007.
Raymond A. Winbush	*Should America Pay?: Slavery and the Raging Debate on Reparations.* New York, NY: Amistad, 2003.
Thom Winckelmann	*Human Trafficking.* Yankton, SD: Erickson Press, 2009.
Yoshiaki Yoshimi	*Comfort Women: Sexual Slavery in the Japanese Military During World War II.* Trans. Suzanne O'Brien. New York, NY: Columbia University Press, 2000.

Index

Geographic headings and page numbers in **boldface** refer to viewpoints about that country or region.